I0201786

GODLINESS
IS
PROFITABLE
FOR ALL THINGS

by

Isaac Barrow

(1630-1677)

GODLINESS
IS
PROFITABLE
FOR ALL THINGS

by

Isaac Barrow, D. D.
(1630-1677)

Originally Published
London
1683

2011 Edition

From the 1823 Edition
Edited & updated by Hail & Fire

"Godliness is Profitable for All Things," by Isaac Barrow, originally published in 1683 in two sermons under the title, "The Profitableness of Godliness," is herein reprinted from the 1823 Edition with edits, updates, and additional footnotes and material added by Hail & Fire.

Copyright © 2011 by Hail & Fire
All rights reserved.

ISBN-10 0982804350
ISBN-13 978-0-9828043-5-3

Hail & Fire is a resource for Reformed and Gospel Theology in the works, exhortations, prayers, and apologetics of those who have maintained the Gospel and expounded upon the Scripture as the Eternal Word of God and the sole authority in Christian doctrine.

"By manifestation of the truth commending ourselves to every man's conscience in the sight of God." 2 Corinthians 4:2

www.hailandfire.com

Reseller and Bulk Order Discounts: orders@hailandfire.com

Isaac Barrow

1630-1677

The following text is taken from two sermons by Isaac Barrow, D. D., who was Master of Trinity College at Cambridge from 1672 until his death in 1677. Prior to his being appointed to this position by Charles II, he held a Greek Professorship and the Lucasian Chair of Mathematics at Cambridge. It was his friend and former pupil, Isaac Newton, who succeeded to this chair after he chose to devote himself entirely to divinity.

The works of Isaac Barrow, were, upon his death, presented by his father, Thomas Barrow, to Heneage, the Earl of Nottingham, Lord High Chancellor of England and member of the King's Privy Council, for the imparting of such works and sermons to the public.

Isaac Barrow is entombed in
Westminster Abbey.

TABLE OF CONTENTS

GODLINESS IS PROFITABLE FOR ALL THINGS

GODLINESS
IS
PROFITABLE
FOR ALL THINGS

PART I

The Profitability of Godliness

MEN ARE GENERALLY DEVOTED TO PROFIT

"But godliness is profitable for all things."
1 Timothy 4:8

By general and unanimous consent all men are devoted to profit as to the immediate goal of all their designs and the purpose of their undertakings! We cannot help but see this if we ponder the activities of men with even the slightest attention, and consider what is acted out upon this theatre of human affairs.

In all labor there is profit: but the talk of the lips tends only to poverty," Proverbs 14:23.

All that we see men so very serious and industrious about, that is, business—that which they trudge for in the streets, which they work or wait for in the shops, which they meet and crowd for at the exchange, which they sue for in the hall and solicit for at the court, which they plow and dig for, which they march and fight for in the field, which they travel for at land, and sail for, chancing shipwreck on rocks and in storms upon the sea, which they study hard for with diligence in private and dispute for in the schools, and yes, which they frequently pray for and preach about in the church—what is it but profit?

Is it not, most apparently, profit for which men so eagerly contest one with another and quarrel, and so bitterly envy and emulate, so fiercely clamor and inveigh, so cunningly supplant and undermine one another? Is it not profit that fills their hearts with mutual hatred and spite, which arms their tongues with slander and reproach like the tip of a blade, and which often imbrues their hands in blood and slaughter, for which also they expose life and limb to danger? Is it not profit for which they undergo grievous toils and drudgeries, for which they distract their mind with cares, and "pierce their heart with sorrows."[1] Is it not profit to which they sacrifice their present ease and contentment, yes, to which commonly they prostitute their honor and conscience?

If you take note of it, profit, you will see, is the great mistress, which is wooed and courted by all men everywhere with such passionate rivalry. Profit is the common mark upon which all eyes are focused and all efforts are aimed, and all endeavors

---

1. "For the love of money is the root of all evil: which while some coveted after, they have erred from the faith, and pierced themselves through with many sorrows," 1 Timothy 6:10.

strike at. This is the wage that men demand for all their pains, the prize they hope for all their combats, the harvest they seek from all the year's assiduous labor. This is the bait by which you may entice and seduce most men to go anywhere, and the most certain sign by which you may predict what any man will do: mark where his profit is and there you will find him. This some seek professedly and with open face, others slyly and under a thin veil of pretence—under guise of friendship, of love to public good, of loyalty, or of some religious zeal they seek it; some directly and in a plain track, others obliquely and by subtle artifice; some by sordid and base means, others in ways more cleanly and laudably; some gravely and modestly, others wildly and furiously. All, with very few exceptions, in one manner or another, in most of their proceedings clearly level[1] and drive at it.

This practice then being so common, and seeing that men are reasonable creatures, the fact then that their ends and desires and motivations are so focused toward profiting in all their endeavors surely cannot proceed from mere brutishness or imbecility. There must be some semblance of reason that draws men to and drives them forward in this manner. And the reason is obvious indeed and it is evident enough—the very term *profit* implies it. Profit itself signifies that which is useful and conducive to all those purposes that are really or seemingly good. The gain of money or of something

---

1. Take aim; the mark at which we level.

equivalent to it is therefore specially called profit because it readily supplies that which is lacking for every necessity, it furnishes that which is needed for every convenience, and it feeds every pleasure, satisfies every fancy and curiosity, promotes ease and liberty, supports honor and dignity, procures power, dependencies, and friendships, and renders every man someone considerable in the world. In fine, profit enables each man to do good and to perform works of beneficence and charity. Profit is therefore so much boasted of and so much pursued because, for each of us, it is able or seems able to procure or promote some desirable good in our lives.

If therefore some project should be proposed to us that seems quite feasible and it is probable that it will succeed, so that, in the pursuance of it we are assured that we will obtain great profit, it is consistent with our own nature, even our own selves, and it is conformable to our usual manner of behaving, that we should be very ready to embrace and execute such a project. And such a project it is that is proposed in my text, which is also attested by a very trusty voucher[1] and one who is a skilful judge of such things, who had himself fully experimented it. This proposal is in itself very practical, so that any of us may, if we have a mind to it and will trouble ourselves regarding it, thoroughly extending ourselves to carry it through, it will exceedingly turn to our account and bring in

---

1. Witness.

gains for us as are unspeakably vast. In comparison to that which is spoken in the text, all other designs that men pursue with so much care and toil, are either very unprofitable and detrimental, yielding only shadows of that which is true profit, or they do real damage to us inasmuch as we set our hearts upon them as the true and real profit that we are to pursue or attain in this world.

THE PROPOSAL: THAT THE PRACTICE OF PIETY IS PROFITABLE

"Godliness is profitable for all things."
1 Timothy 4:8

The proposal that is contained in this text is briefly this: to be religious or pious, that is, to believe in our minds steadfastly upon God, not after our own imaginations, but as nature in some measure and revelation more clearly declares him, and to earnestly love and reverence him in our hearts, and in all our practice sincerely and diligently to observe his laws, this is that which St. Paul affirms to be "profitable for all things." It is my intent, by God's help, to recommend this to you, demonstrating that it really is so by representing some of those numberless benefits and advantages that accrue from piety or the practice of godliness, and extend to all conditions and capacities of men, to all states, all seasons, and in effect to all affairs of life.

The obstruction to the practice of piety is blindness to the profit thereof.

It has always been a primary obstruction to the practice of piety that piety has been taken for no friend, or rather, for an enemy of profit, even as being both unprofitable and prejudicial to its followers. Many are the forms and shades of argument that contain and countenance that opinion. For religion in many ways seems to smother or to slacken the industry and alacrity of men in following after profit, by charging them to be content with a little, "Let your conversation be without covetousness; and be content with such things as you have: for he has said, I will never leave thee, nor forsake thee," Hebrews 13:5; and to be careful for nothing, "Be careful for nothing; but in everything by prayer and supplication with thanksgiving let your requests be made known unto God," Philippians 4:6. By diverting their affections and cares from worldly affairs to matters of another nature, place, and time, prescribing first above all that men seek things spiritual, heavenly, and future, "If you then be risen with Christ, seek those things which are above, where Christ sits on the right hand of God," Colossians 3:1.

By disparaging all secular wealth, as a thing that is very mean and unimportant in comparison to virtue and spiritual goods; by rebuking greedy desires and aspiring thoughts after the wealth of this present world; by debarring the most ready ways of getting wealth, that is, violence, exaction, fraud, and flattery. Yea, and by narrowing and straightening the best ways, that is, eager care and diligence, and by commending strict justice in all cases, always taking the side of conscience when it clashes with self-interest. Even by paring away at the primary uses of wealth, through the prohibition of its free enjoyment, the pride associated with the possession of it, and the pleasures to be gotten by it; by enjoining liberality in charity and mercy and by engaging men to expose their goods sometimes to imminent hazard, sometimes to certain loss, obliging them to forsake all things, and to embrace poverty if need be for the sake of preserving piety.

It seems favorable to this conceit that religion stifles profitableness, to observe that often bad men do appear to thrive and prosper through impious courses, while good men seem, on account of their goodness, to suffer or to be nothing visibly better for it when they endure much hardship and distress because of their faith. "There is a just man that perishes in his righteousness, and there is a wicked man that prolongs his life in his wickedness," Ecclesiastes 7:15.[1]

And it furthers this prejudice that some persons, void of true piety, or imperfectly religious—that is, those dabblers in religion—do not from their lame,

---

1. The full text is: "In the day of prosperity be joyful, but in the day of adversity consider: God also hath set the one over against the other, to the end that man should find nothing after him. All things have I seen in the days of my vanity: there is a just man that perisheth in his righteousness, and there is a wicked man that prolongeth his life in his wickedness," Ecclesiastes 7:14-15.

slight, and superficial performances in religion and piety, feel satisfactory returns according to that which they supposed they would find.[1] Thus, to the defamation of piety, such persons are apt to say, with those men of whom the prophet speaks, "It is vain to serve God; and what profit is it that we have kept his ordinance, and that we have walked mournfully before the Lord of hosts?" Malachi 3:14. Yea, and we know that sometimes very pious men, being in an ill humor or somewhat agitated by the urgent pressures of affliction and the disappointments and crosses incident to all men here in this realm of trouble, are apt to complain and express themselves dissatisfied, saying with Job, "It profits a man nothing that he should delight himself with God. What advantage will it be unto me, and what profit shall I have, if I be cleansed from my sin?"[2] Or with David, "Verily, I have cleansed my heart in vain, and washed my hands in

---

1. "No one expects to attain to the height of learning, power, wealth or military glory without vigorous resolution, strenuous diligence and steady perseverance. Yet we expect to be Christians without labor, study, or inquiry. This is the more preposterous as Christianity *(is)* a revelation from God," William Wilberforce, *Real Christianity* (1797).

2. These are the words that Elihu puts into Job's mouth (Job 34:9 & 35:3), but what Job actually said was, "He has cast me into the mire, and I am become like dust and ashes. I cry unto thee, and thou dost not hear me: I stand up, and thou regardest me not. Thou art become cruel to me: with thy strong hand thou opposest thyself against me," Job 30:19-21. This he said when he struggled in his dilemma for the reason that God should cause such distress to fall upon him when it was abhorrent to his very soul to wish evil upon even his enemy or to refuse to succor those in distress or need, or to neglect any duty of religion or faith toward God, which he practiced from the heart.

innocency: for all the day long I have been plagued, and chastened every morning."[1]

To these considerations, in some respects disadvantageous to piety as they are, may be added, that the constant and certain profits arising from the practice of piety—although incomparably more substantial and more sensible than any other form of profit to the mind that is stayed upon faith toward God—are yet not large enough or palpable enough that men, who from being immersed in earth and flesh are blinded in their error, dull in their apprehension, vain and inconsiderate in their judgments, tainted and vitiated in their palates, can discern their worth or relish their sweetness.[2]

---

1. This Psalm is generally ascribed to Asaph, who prefaced his comments saying, "But as for me, my feet were almost gone; my steps had well nigh slipped. For I was envious at the foolish, when I saw the prosperity of the wicked," Psalms 73:2-3. It is in this state of mind, before he considered the end of those who practice unrighteousness, that is, "Until I went into the sanctuary of God; then understood I their end. Surely thou didst set them in slippery places: thou castedst them down into destruction," Psalms 73:17-18, until he considered that the unbelieving are lulled into complacency by the very lack of that disciplining hand of God upon them and the very prosperity that God blesses them with in this world, never regard God or seek him in earnest, and thus deliver themselves up to destruction.

2. "A hard heart now makes heaven and hell seem but trifles. We have showed them everlasting glory and misery, and they are as men asleep; our words are as stones cast against a wall, which fly back in our faces. We talk of terrible things, but it is to dead men; we search the wounds, but they never feel it; we speak to rocks rather than to men; the earth will as soon tremble as they. But when these dead souls are revived, what passionate sensibility, what working affections, what pangs of horror, what depths of sorrow will there then be! How violently will they denounce and reproach themselves! How will they rage against their former madness! The lamentations of the most affectionate wife for the loss of her husband, or of

Hence it is that so many follow the judgment and practice of those of whom Job speaks, who "say unto God, Depart from us; for we desire not the knowledge of your ways. What is the Almighty, that we should serve him? And what profit should we have, if we pray unto him?" Job 21:14-15.

The innumerable advantages by which the profitableness of piety may be seen.

Leaving these prejudices and the recommendation of St. Paul's admonition, I shall propose some of those innumerable advantages by the consideration of which the immense profitableness of piety may be clearly seen. First, I shall mention those considerations that plainly import universality in the advantages of piety, and then I shall touch upon some of the benefits of piety that seem more particular in scope, yet in effect are vastly large and of very widespread influence.

I.
Piety is exceedingly useful.

First then, we may consider that piety is exceedingly useful to all sorts of men, in all capacities, all states, all relations; fitting and disposing them to manage all their respective

---

the tenderest mother for the loss of her children, will be nothing to theirs for the loss of heaven." Rev. Richard Baxter, *The Saint's Everlasting Rest.*

concernments, and to discharge all their peculiar duties, in a proper, just, and decent manner.

Piety renders all superiors equal and moderate in their administrations; mild, courteous, and affable in their associations; and benign and condescending in their demeanor toward their inferiors. "You masters, do the same things unto them, forbearing threatening: knowing that your Master also is in heaven; neither is there respect of persons with him," Ephesians 6:9. "Masters, give unto your servants that which is just and equal; knowing that you also have a Master in heaven," Colossians 4:1.

Correspondingly, piety disposes inferiors to be sincere and faithful, modest, loving, respectful, diligent, and apt to willingly yield due subjection and service. "Servants, obey in all things your masters according to the flesh; not with eyeservice, as menpleasers; but in singleness of heart, fearing God: and whatsoever ye do, do it heartily, as to the Lord, and not unto men; knowing that of the Lord you shall receive the reward of the inheritance: for you serve the Lord Christ," Colossians 3:22-24. "Servants, be subject to your masters with all fear," 1 Peter 2:18.

Piety inclines princes to be just, gentle, benign, careful for their subjects' good, apt to administer justice uprightly, to protect that which is right, to encourage virtue, and to rebuke wickedness.

Answerably, piety renders subjects loyal, submissive, obedient, quiet, and peaceable, ready to yield due honor, to pay the tributes and bear the burdens imposed, to discharge all duties and observe all laws prescribed by their governors, conscionably, patiently, cheerfully, without reluctance, grudging, or murmuring.[1]

Piety makes parents loving, gentle, and cautious for their children's good education and comfortable subsistence. "You fathers, provoke not your children to wrath: but bring them up in the nurture and admonition of the Lord," Ephesians 6:4. "Fathers, provoke not your children to anger, lest they be discouraged," Colossians 3:21.[2]

In turn, piety renders children dutiful, respectful, grateful, and apt to requite their parents. "Children, obey your parents in all things: for this is well pleasing unto the Lord," Colossians 3:20. "Children, obey your parents in the Lord: for this is right. Honor thy father and mother; (which is the first commandment with promise;) that it may be well with thee, and thou mayest live long on the earth," Ephesians 6:1-3. "Let them learn (to) show

---

1. "Let every soul be subject unto the higher powers. For there is no power but of God: the powers that be are ordained of God," Romans 13:1; "Put them in mind to be subject to principalities and powers, to obey magistrates, to be ready to every good work," Titus 3:1; "Submit yourselves to every ordinance of man for the Lord's sake: whether it be to the king, as supreme; or unto governors, as unto them that are sent by him for the punishment of evildoers, and for the praise of them that do well," 1 Peter 2:13-14; also 1 Peter 4:9, & Philippians 2:14.

2. Also, 1 Timothy 5:8.

piety at home, and to requite their parents: for that is good and acceptable before God," 1 Timothy 5:4.

Husbands, from piety, become affectionate and yielding to their wives; through which also the wives are rendered more submissive and obedient to their husbands. "Wives, submit yourselves unto your own husbands, as unto the Lord. For the husband is the head of the wife, even as Christ is the head of the church: and he is the savior of the body. Therefore as the church is subject unto Christ, so let the wives be to their own husbands in everything," Ephesians 5:22-24. "Wives, submit yourselves unto your own husbands, as it is fit in the Lord. Husbands, love your wives, and be not bitter against them," Colossians 3:18-19.[1] "Likewise, you husbands, dwell with them according to knowledge, giving honor unto the wife, as unto the weaker vessel, and as being heirs together of the grace of life; that your prayers be not hindered," 1 Peter 3:7.[2]

---

1. Also, "Teach the young women to be sober, to love their husbands, to love their children, To be discreet, chaste, keepers at home, good, obedient to their own husbands, that the Word of God be not blasphemed," Titus 2:4-5; & "For after this manner in the old time the holy women also, who trusted in God, adorned themselves, being in subjection unto their own husbands," 1 Peter 3:5.

2. "Godliness is profitable unto all things, having promise of the life that now is, and of that which is to come. The same principle of divine grace that unites us to God will bind us closer to each other. Religion contains in it not only the seeds of immortal virtues, but also those that are mortal. Not only the buds of excellences that are to flourish in the temple of heaven, but also those that grow up in the house of our pilgrimage upon earth, to enliven with their beauty and to refresh the family circle with their fragrance. A good

Piety disposes friends to be friends indeed, full of cordial affection and good-will, entirely faithful, firmly constant, industriously careful and active in performing all the good offices of friendship mutually.[1]

Piety engages men to be diligent in their calling, faithful to their trusts, content and peaceable in their employment and occupation, and thereby serviceable to the public good. "Whatsoever you do, do it heartily, as to the Lord, and not unto men," Colossians 3:23. "Seest thou a man diligent in his business? He shall stand before kings; he shall not stand before mean men," Proverbs 22:29.

Piety renders all men just and punctual in their dealing, orderly and quiet in their behavior, courteous, civil, and polite in their conversation, friendly and charitable upon all occasions, apt to assist, to relieve, and to comfort one another. "Bear ye one another's burdens, and so fulfill the law of Christ," Galatians 6:2. "As we have therefore opportunity, let us do good unto all men, especially unto them who are of the household of faith," Galatians 6:10.[2]

Christian cannot be a bad husband or father and, as this is equally true in everything, he who has the most piety will shine the most in all the relationships of life." Rev. John Angell James, *The Marriage Ring*.

1. "A friend loves at all times, and a brother is born for adversity," Proverbs 17:17.

2. Also, "Whatsoever things are true, whatsoever things are honest, whatsoever things are just, whatsoever things are pure, whatsoever things are lovely, whatsoever things are of good report; if there be any virtue, and if there be any praise, think on these things,"

Piety ties all relations more firmly and strongly, confirming and augmenting all endearments. It enforces and establishes all obligations by the firm cords of conscience. Set aside piety and no engagement can hold sure against temptations of interest or pleasure. So much difference is there between the performance of these duties out of a natural temper, or fear of punishment, or hope of temporal reward, selfish design, regard to credit, or any other similar principles, and the discharging of them out of a religious conscience.[1] It is a pure and religious conscience alone that will keep men bound one to another, uniform in their designs, resolute in their responsibilities one to another, and stable in all their duties and undertakings. Whereas, on the contrary, all other principles are loose and slippery, and will soon be shaken and falter when such a person is tempted regarding his interests and the gratification of some thing by which he is in expectation of some good or enjoyable pleasure.

In consequence of those practices that spring from piety, it displaces oppression, violence, faction, disorder, and murmurings, banishing them out of the state; schisms and scandals out of the church; pride and haughtiness, sloth and luxury, detraction, and sycophantry out of the court; corruption and

---

Philippians 4:8; "The Lord make you to increase and abound in love one toward another, and toward all men, even as we do toward you: to the end he may stablish your hearts unblameable in holiness before God," 1 Thessalonians 3:12-13.

1. "Thou shalt love thy neighbor as thyself," Mark 12:31, and "Love works no ill to his neighbor: therefore love is the fulfilling of the law," Romans 13:10.

partiality out of the judiciary; clamors and tumults out of the street; brawling, grudges, and jealousies out of families; extortion, artifice, and cheating out of trade; and strife, emulation, slanderous backbiting, and bitter and foul language out of conversation. In all places and in all societies, piety produces, advances, and establishes order, peace, safety, prosperity, and all that is good, all that is lovely and agreeable, and all that is convenient and pleasant for human society and ordinary life.

Piety is that which, as the wise Solomon says, exalts a nation, and piety is that which establishes any position of power, rule, or authority: "Righteousness exalts a nation," Proverbs 14:34; "It is an abomination to kings to commit wickedness: for the throne is established by righteousness," Proverbs 16:12; and "The king that faithfully judges the poor, his throne shall be established forever," Proverbs 29:14. Wisdom and understanding speak: "Counsel is mine, and sound wisdom: I am understanding; I have strength. By me kings reign, and princes decree justice. By me princes rule, and nobles, even all the judges of the earth," Proverbs 8:14-16.

Piety is indeed the best foundation and the best security or preservation there can be of government and of the commonweal, because it fixes and establishes the political body in a sound constitution of health, it firmly cements the parts thereof together; it puts all things into their proper order and places all things upon a steady and a constant course. Piety procures mutual respect and affection between governors and citizens, from which goodwill arises our very safety, ease, and mutual gratification, with the expectation of good imparted to and arising from both one to another. Piety renders men *truly* good—that is, truly and from the heart just and honest, sober and considerate, modest and peaceable. And therefore, the practice of piety renders men apt without any constraint of necessity or conflict of passions, to yield each one their due, one to another, in every facet of ordinary life, of society, and of government. Piety is not moved to needless change, and it does not disposed men to raise any disturbance. Piety puts men in a good humor and it sustains them in it, preserving that good and decent disposition of mind, whereupon all things pass smoothly and pleasantly among men. Piety cherishes worth, and encourages industry, whereupon virtue flourishes and wealth is increased and, as a result, the occasions and means of disorder are stopped and the pretenses for sedition and faction are cut off.

In fine, piety most certainly procures the benediction, *the blessing,* of God, who is the source of all the enjoyment of peace and prosperity. And whereby we say with the great politician Solomon, "When it goes well with the righteous, the city rejoices," Proverbs 11:10; and "When the righteous are in authority, the people rejoice," Proverbs 29:2.

Piety is therefore the concernment of all men, who, as the Psalmist says, desire to live well, "What man is he that desires life, and loves many days, that he may see good? Keep thy tongue from evil, and thy lips from speaking guile. Depart from evil, and do good; seek peace, and pursue it," Psalms 34:12-14. Piety is the concernment of all who would be pleased to see good days, "For he that will love life, and see good days, let him refrain his tongue from evil, and his lips that they speak no guile: Let him eschew evil, and do good; let him seek peace, and ensue it," 1 Peter 3:10-11.

Piety is the special interest of every great person—of the civil magistrates, of them that govern in the highest offices, of those who are set above others either in education or in opportunity, and of all persons that have any considerable interest in the governing, administration, and education of the world. For, whoever would safely and sweetly enjoy their dignity, power, or wealth, must by all means be concerned in the protection and promotion of piety as the best instrument of their security and the undisturbed enjoyment of the conveniences of their position or state in this world.

Piety is, in all respects, their greatest wisdom and policy; it will both preserve their outward state here in this world, as well as satisfy their consciences and save their souls in the hereafter. All the Machiavellian arts and tricks, all the sleights and fetches[1] of worldly craft, do amount to nothing in comparison to this one plain and easy way of securing and furthering their interests.

If it would be a gross absurdity to desire some particular fruits, and not to take care what plant is cultivated or not to cultivate the stock that will yield the desired fruit, then it is an equal absurdity that any reasonable man should look to gain those good tempers and tendencies that proceed from piety alone without striving to further piety among all men. If every prince gladly would have his subjects loyal and obedient, every governor would have the people honest, diligent, and observant, if every parent would have his children obliging and grateful, every man would have his friend faithful and kind, if everyone would have those with whom he must negotiate and converse act in a just and sincere manner, if anyone would choose to be related to such as are just and sincere and would esteem their relations to such persons to be happiness itself, then consequently we must, every man, strive to further piety from which all these good dispositions and practices do singularly proceed.

II.
Piety fits a man for all conditions.

Piety fits a man for all conditions, qualifying

---

1.   A stratagem by which one thing seems intended and another is done.

him to pass through them all with the best advantage, wisely, cheerfully, and safely, so that he might incur no considerable harm or detriment by them, whatever they might be.

Is a man prosperous, high, or wealthy in condition? Piety will guard him from all the mischiefs incident to that state, and it will dispose him to enjoy the best advantages thereof. Piety will keep him from being high minded and puffed up with vain conceit and from being transported with gratification and confidence in his wealth. Piety will remind him that all that he has is purely the gift of God and that it depends absolutely upon God's disposal, so that, as it was given to him so also it may be taken from him. It will teach him that he cannot securely retain wealth and estate other than by humility, by gratitude, and by the good use of his wealth.[1] Piety will remind him also, that he shall assuredly be brought to render a strict account concerning the good management of all that he was entrusted with in this world.[2] It will preserve him from being perverted or corrupted with the temptations to which that condition is most liable, that is, from luxury, from sloth, from

---

1. "He that has a bountiful eye shall be blessed; for he gives of his bread to the poor," Proverbs 22:9; and "Charge them that are rich in this world, that they be not highminded, nor trust in uncertain riches, but in the living God, who gives us richly all things to enjoy; that they do good, that they be rich in good works, ready to distribute, willing to communicate; laying up in store for themselves a good foundation against the time to come, that they may lay hold on eternal life," 1 Timothy 6:17-19.
2. "Go to now, you rich men, etc.," James 5:1-5.

stupidity, and from forgetfulness of God and of himself; it will maintain him in a sober and steady mind among the floods of plenty. Piety is as a fence around him, protecting him from insolence and proud contempt of others, and rendering him civil, condescending, kind and helpful to those who are in a less advantageous state. Piety instructs and incites him to apply his wealth and power to the best uses, to the service of God, to the benefit of his neighbor, for the bettering of his own reputation, and his most solid comfort.[1] Piety is the right ballast[2] of prosperity, the only antidote for the inconveniencies of wealth;[3] it is that which secures, sweetens, and sanctifies all good things, so that, without it, all things that seem good are in truth very noxious or extremely perilous.[4] Riches, power,

---

1. "Let the brother of low degree rejoice in that he is exalted: But the rich, in that he is made low: because as the flower of the grass he shall pass away. For the sun is no sooner risen with a burning heat, but it withers the grass, and the flower thereof falls, and the grace of the fashion of it perishes: so also shall the rich man fade away in his ways," James 1:9-11.

2. That which is used, as ballast in a ship, to make a thing steady.

3. For example, "Wealth makes many friends," Proverbs 19:4; "Many will entreat the favor of the prince," Proverbs 19:6; "The rich man's wealth is his strong city, and as an high wall in his own conceit," Proverbs 18:11; and "Surely men of low degree are vanity, and men of high degree are a lie: to be laid in the balance, they are altogether lighter than vanity. Trust not in oppression, and become not vain in robbery: if riches increase, set not your heart upon them," Psalms 62:9-10.

4. "The labor of the righteous tends to life: the fruit of the wicked to sin," Proverbs 10:16, and "Better is little with the fear of the Lord than great treasure and trouble therewith. Better is a dinner of herbs where love is, than a stalled ox and hatred therewith," Proverbs 15:16-17.

honor, ease, and pleasure are so many poisons or so many snares without piety.[1]

Again, is a man poor and low in the world? Piety improves and sweetens even that state. It keeps his spirits up and it keeps him from dejection, desperation, and disconsolateness. It frees him from all grievous uneasiness of mind and anxiety of heart, showing him that although he seems to have little, yet he may be assured that he shall lack nothing—he having a most certain succor and never-failing supply from God's good providence that, notwithstanding the present straightness of his condition or the scantiness of outward things, he has a title to those goods that are infinitely more precious and more considerable. A pious man in such a straight cannot but apprehend himself to be like the child of a most wealthy, kind, and careful father, who, although he has yet nothing in his own possession, or passing to his name from his father, yet he is assured that he can never come into any want of what is needed and necessary to him.[2] The Lord of all things—who has all things in heaven

---

1. "Prosperity, worldly success, outward enjoyments, riches, honors—try men's hearts and reveal their thoughts. Some may fancy the fire of prosperity to be designed rather for comfort than for trial, rather to compose, than to search us; but scarcely anything more clearly demonstrates the falseness or soundness of religion; it is to grace, what fire is to gold. Particularly, it occasions an exhibition of the self-flattery and delusion of those who have had a name to live, while dead; and of the unequivocal evidences of true religion, in real saints." Rev. John Flavel, *The Touchstone of Christian Sincerity*.

2. "Let your conversation be without covetousness; and be content with such things as you have: for he has said, I will never leave thee, nor forsake thee. So that we may boldly say, The Lord is my helper, and I will not fear what man shall do unto me," Hebrews 13:5-6.

and earth at his disposal, who is infinitely tender regarding his children's good and does incessantly watch over them—being his gracious Father, how can that pious man fear to be left destitute, or not to be competently provided for, as is truly best for him according to the care that God has toward us?

And here is the difference between a pious and an impious man. Is the pious man in need? He has then an invisible refuge to fly to, an invisible store to furnish him; he has something beyond all these present things to hope in and to comfort himself with. Whereas the impious person has nothing beside present appearances to support or solace himself by, which things, when they fail, down he sinks into dejection and despair.[1] Is the good man in affliction? He knows that when affliction comes, it does not come upon him without God's wise appointment nor without good intention toward him. He knows that affliction comes for probation, exercise, and improvement of his virtues, or for wholesome correction of his bad dispositions. He knows that affliction is only a medicine and a

---

1. "Labor to see an excellency in the power of godliness, a beauty in the life of Christ. If the means of grace have a loveliness in them, surely grace itself has much more; for, the goodness of the means lies in its suitableness and serviceableness to the end; the form of godliness has no goodness in it any farther than it aids and becomes useful to the soul in the power and practice of godliness. The life of holiness is the only excellent life, it is the life of saints and angels in heaven; yea, it is the life of God in himself. As it is a great proof of the baseness and filthiness of sin, that sinners seek to cover it; so it is a great proof of the excellency of godliness, that so many pretend to it. The very hypocrite's fair profession pleads the cause of religion, although the hypocrite is then really worst, when he is seemingly best." Rev. Matthew Mead, *The Almost Christian Discovered.*

discipline to him, which shall have a comfortable conclusion and end.[1] He knows that it shall last no longer than it is expedient for him that it should last, and because of which, he patiently submits to it and undergoes it cheerfully, with the same mind wherewith a patient will swallow down an unsavory dose of medicine that he believes is conducive to his need and his health.[2] Never, indeed, has any man enjoyed more real contentment or has been more truly satisfied than good men have been in a seeming depth of adversity. What men upon this earth have ever been more sorely afflicted, have undergone greater losses, disgraces, labors, troubles, and distresses of every kind than the holy Apostles did? Yet, they did most heartily rejoice and exult and triumph in them all. Such a wondrous virtue piety has that it is able to change all things into

---

1. "Our faithful and good Shepherd affords to us," says John Newton, "strength according to our day. He knows our frame, and will lay no more on us than he will enable us to bear; yea, I trust, no more than he will cause to work for our good." "Our comforts," he continues, "of every kind come free and undeserved. But, when we are afflicted, it is because there is a need for it. He does it not willingly. Our trials are either salutary medicines, or honorable appointments, to put us in such circumstances as may best qualify us to show forth his praise." Rev. John Newton, *Works.*

2. "In the covenant of grace, God has engaged himself to keep you from the evils, snares, and the temptations of this world; in the covenant of grace, God has engaged himself to purge away your sins, to brighten and increase your graces, to crucify your hearts to the world, and to prepare you and preserve you to his heavenly kingdom. Consider also that by afflictions he effects all this according to his covenant: 'If his children forsake my law, and walk not in my commandments; if they break my statutes, and keep not my commandments, (Then will I visit their transgression with the rod, and their iniquity with stripes. Nevertheless my lovingkindness will I not utterly take from him, nor suffer my faithfulness to fail).' Psalms 89:30-33." Rev. Thomas Brooks, *The Mute Christian.*

matter of consolation and joy.[1] In effect, no condition can be evil or sad to a pious man: his very sorrows are pleasant, his infirmities are wholesome, his wants enrich him, his disgraces adorn him, his burdens ease him, his duties are privileges, when he falls he finds the grounds of advancement, his very sins breeding, as they do, contrition, humility, circumspection, and vigilance, do only better and profit him. Impiety, on the other hand, spoils every condition, corrupts and degrades all good things, and embitters all the conveniences and comforts of this life.[2]

III.
Piety comprises within itself all other profit.

Piety does comprise within itself virtually all other profits, serving all the design of all of them: whatever kind of desirable good we could hope to find in any other form of profit, we may assuredly enjoy in the fruits of piety.

He that has piety is *ipso facto* vastly rich already. He is entitled to immense treasures of

---

1. "What God wills is best, Hebrews 12:10. When he wills sickness, sickness is better than health; when he wills weakness, weakness is better than strength; when he wills want, want is better than wealth; when he wills reproach, reproach is better than honor; when he wills death, death is better than life. As God is wisdom itself, and so knows that which is best, so he is goodness itself, and therefore cannot do anything but that which is best: therefore hold your peace." Rev. Thomas Brooks, *The Mute Christian.*

2. Proverbs 4 - "Wisdom is the principal thing; therefore get wisdom: and with all thy getting get understanding. Exalt her, and she shall promote thee: she shall bring thee to honor, etc."

most precious wealth, in comparison to which, all the gold and all the jewels in the world are mere baubles.[1] He has interest in God and can call God his—God who is the all and in regard to whom all things that exist are less than nothing. The infinite power and wisdom of God belong to him, to be ever and upon all fit occasions, employed for his benefit. All the inestimable treasures of heaven, a place infinitely rich, are his after this moment of life, to have and to hold forever. With great reason the wise Solomon said that, "In the house of the righteous is much treasure," Proverbs 15:6. Piety therefore is profitable, as immediately investing a man in wealth and whereas the desired fruits of profit are principally honor, power, pleasure, safety, liberty, ease, the opportunity of getting knowledge, and the means of benefiting others. All these, we shall see, do abundantly accrue from piety, and in truth proceed only from piety.

The pious man is in truth most honorable, *Inter homines pro summo est optimus*, says Seneca.[2] Solomon speaks thus: "The righteous is more excellent than his neighbor," Proverbs 12:26. He is dignified by the most illustrious titles, a son of God, a friend and favorite to the sovereign King

---

1. "I count all things but loss for the excellency of the knowledge of Christ Jesus my Lord: for whom I have suffered the loss of all things, and do count them but dung, that I may win Christ, and be found in him, not having mine own righteousness, which is of the law, but that which is through the faith of Christ, the righteousness which is of God by faith," Philippians 3:8-9.
2. Seneca. *Ep. xc.*

of the world, an heir of heaven, a denizen[1] of the Jerusalem that is above[2]—titles far surpassing all those that worldly state assumes.[3] He is approved by the best and most infallible judgments, wherein true honor resides. He is respected by God himself, by the holy angels, by the blessed saints, by all good and all wise persons, yea, commonly by all men, for the effects of genuine piety are so venerable and amiable that scarcely can any man do otherwise in his heart than much esteem him that practices them.

The pious man is also the most potent man: he has a kind of omnipotence, because he can do whatever he will, that is, whatever he ought to do[4] and because the divine power is ever ready to assist him in his pious enterprises, so that he can do all things by Christ that strengthens him.[5] He is able to combat and vanquish him that is ο ισχυγος, '

---

1. A stranger that is admitted to residence and certain rights in a foreign country.

2. "But Jerusalem which is above is free, which is the mother of us all," Galatians 4:26.

3. "Henceforth I call you not servants; for the servant knows not what his lord does: but I have called you friends; for all things that I have heard of my Father I have made known unto you," John 15:15; "Behold, what manner of love the Father has bestowed upon us, that we should be called the sons of God," 1 John 3:1; and "(Jesus Christ) has made us kings and priests unto God and his Father," Revelation 1:6.

4. "Knowing this, that our old man is crucified with him, that the body of sin might be destroyed, that henceforth we should not serve sin," Romans 6:6.

5. "I have learned, in whatsoever state I am, therewith to be content. I know both how to be abased, and I know how to abound: everywhere and in all things I am instructed both to be full and to be hungry, both to abound and to suffer need. I can do all things through Christ which strengthens me," Philippians 4:11-13.

the stout and mighty one, to wage war with happy success against principalities and powers.[1] He conquers and commands himself, which is the bravest victory and noblest empire:[2] he quells fleshly lusts, subdues inordinate passions, and repels strong temptations. He, through his faith, overcomes the world[3] with a conquest far more glorious than any that an Alexander the Great or a Caesar could gain. He, in fine, performs the most worthy exploits and deserves the most honorable triumphs. "For when you were the servants of sin, you were free from righteousness. What fruit had you then in those things whereof you are now ashamed? For the end of those things is death. But now being made free from sin, and become servants to God, you have your fruit unto holiness, and the end everlasting life. For the wages of sin is death; but the gift of God is eternal life through Jesus Christ our Lord," Romans 6:20-23. "In all things we are more than conquerors through him that loved us," Romans 8:37.

---

1. "For we wrestle not against flesh and blood, but against principalities, against powers, against the rulers of the darkness of this world, against spiritual wickedness in high places. Wherefore take unto you the whole armor of God, that ye may be able to withstand in the evil day, and having done all, to stand," Ephesians 6:12-13.

2. "He that is slow to anger is better than the mighty; and he that rules his spirit than he that takes a city," Proverbs 16:32, and inversely, "He that hath no rule over his own spirit is like a city that is broken down, and without walls," Proverbs 25:28.

3. "For whatsoever is born of God overcomes the world: and this is the victory that overcomes the world, even our faith. Who is he that overcomes the world, but he that believes that Jesus is the Son of God?" 1 John 5:4-5.

The pious man enjoys the only true pleasures; hearty, pure, solid, durable pleasures; such pleasures as those of which the divine Psalmist sings: "In thy presence is fullness of joy; at thy right hand there are pleasures forevermore," Psalms 16:11. That "all joy in believing,"[1] that "rejoicing of hope," Hebrews 3:6; that incessant "rejoicing in the Lord,"[2] and "greatly delighting in his law,"[3] "his delight is in the law of the Lord; and in his law doth he meditate day and night," Psalms 1:2. That continual feast of a good conscience, that serving the Lord with gladness, "Serve the Lord with gladness: come before his presence with singing," Psalms 100:2. That exceeding gladness with God's countenance,[4] that comfort of the Holy Spirit,[5] that joy unspeakable and full of glory, "Whom having not seen, you love; in whom, though now

---

1. "The God of hope fill you with all joy and peace in believing, that ye may abound in hope, through the power of the Holy Spirit," Romans 15:13.
2. "Rejoice in the Lord always: and again I say, Rejoice," Philippians 4:4.
3. "Praise ye the Lord. Blessed is the man that fears the Lord, that delights greatly in his commandments," Psalms 112:1. "I will delight myself in thy statutes: I will not forget thy Word," Psalms 119:16, "Thy testimonies also are my delight and my counselors," Psalms 119:24, also Psalms 119:47, 70, 77, 92, 111, and "Trouble and anguish have taken hold on me: yet thy commandments are my delights," Psalms 119:143
4. "Thou hast made him most blessed forever: thou hast made him exceeding glad with thy countenance," Psalms 21:6; "The meek also shall increase their joy in the Lord, and the poor among men shall rejoice in the Holy One of Israel," Isaiah 29:19; and "Verily, verily, I say unto you, That you shall weep and lament, but the world shall rejoice: and you shall be sorrowful, but your sorrow shall be turned into joy," John 16:20.
5. "For the kingdom of God is not meat and drink; but righteousness, and peace, and joy in the Holy Spirit," Romans 14:17.

you see him not, yet believing, you rejoice with joy unspeakable and full of glory," 1 Peter 1:8. All these are the satisfaction resulting from the contemplation of heavenly truth, from the sense of God's favor and the pardon of his sins, from the influence of God's grace, and from the hopes and anticipation of everlasting bliss. These are pleasures indeed, in comparison to which all other pleasures are no more than brutish sensualities, sordid impurities, superficial touches, transient flashes of delight such as should be insipid and unsavory to a rational appetite, and such as are tinctured with sourness and bitterness and often bring with them painful remorse or qualms of conscience as a consequence.[1] All the pious man's performances of duty and devotion are full of pure satisfaction and delight here in this world, and they shall be rewarded with perfect and endless joy hereafter.

As for safety, the pious man has it most absolute and sure. He is guarded by Almighty power and wisdom and rests under the shadow of God's wings, "Keep me as the apple of the eye, hide me under the shadow of thy wings," Psalms 17:8, and "How excellent is thy lovingkindness, O God! Therefore

---

1. "For what more delightful than to have God the Father and our Lord at peace with us *(reconciliatio)*, than revelation of the truth *(veritatis revelatio)*, than confession of our errors *(errorum recognitio)*, than pardon of the innumerable sins of our past life *(tot retro criminum venia)*? What greater pleasure than distaste of pleasure itself, contempt of all that the world, can give, true liberty *(vera libertas)*, a pure conscience *(conscientia integra)*, a contented life *(vita sufficiens)*, and freedom from all fear of death *(mortis timor nullus)*?" Tertullian, *de Spectaculis (The Shows)*, Chapter XXIX.

the children of men put their trust under the shadow of thy wings," Psalms 36:7.[1] God upholds him with his hand, "Though he fall, he shall not be utterly cast down: for the Lord upholds him with his hand," Psalms 37:24; and "Hold thou me up, and I shall be safe," Psalms 119:11. God orders his steps, so that none of them shall slide, "The steps of a good man are ordered by the Lord: and he delights in his way," Psalms 37:23; "The law of his God is in his heart; none of his steps shall slide," Psalms 37:31; and "Order my steps in thy Word: and let not any iniquity have dominion over me," Psalms 119:133. God maintains his soul in life and "suffers not our feet to be moved," Psalms 66:9; and "I will walk at liberty: for I seek thy precepts," Psalms 119:45. The pious man being, by the grace and mercy of God, guarded from the assaults and impressions of all enemies, from sin and guilt, from the devil, the world, and the flesh, from death and hell, which are our most formidable and in effect, our only dangerous enemies.

As for liberty, the pious man most entirely and truly enjoys liberty. He alone is free from captivity to that cruel tyrant the devil, from the miserable slavery to sin, and from the grievous dominion of lust and passion. He can do what he pleases— having a mind to do only what is good and fit. The

---

1. Also, "Be merciful unto me, O God, be merciful unto me: for my soul trusts in thee: yea, in the shadow of thy wings will I make my refuge, until these calamities be overpast," Psalms 57:1; and "I will abide in thy tabernacle forever: I will trust in the covert of thy wings," Psalms 61:4.

Law, he observes, is worthily called "the perfect law of liberty," James 1:25, and the Lord that he serves claims only to command freemen and friends: "You are my friends," he says, "if you do whatever I command you," John 15:14. "If the Son therefore shall make you free, you shall be free indeed," John 8:36.

And for ease, it is the pious man alone that knows ease, having his mind exempted from the distraction of cares, from the disorder of passions, from anguish of conscience, from the drudgeries and troubles of this world, and from the vexation and disquietude which sin produces. He finds that made good to him that our Lord, when he invited us, did also promise, "Come unto me, all you that labor and are heavy laden, and I will give you rest," Matt 11:28. He feels the truth of those divine assertions, "Thou wilt keep him in perfect peace, whose mind is stayed on thee: because he trusts in thee," Isaiah 26:3; and "Great peace have they which love thy law: and nothing shall offend them," Psalms 119:165.

As for knowledge, the pious man alone does attain it considerably, so as to become truly wise and learned to his purpose.[1] "Evil men," says the wise Solomon himself, who knew well,

---

1. "He has showed thee, Oh man, what is good; and what doth the Lord require of thee, but to do justly, and to love mercy, and to walk humbly with thy God? The Lord's voice cries unto the city, and the man of wisdom shall see thy name: hear ye the rod, and who has appointed it," Micah 6:8-9.

"understand not judgment: but they that seek the Lord understand all things," Proverbs 28:5. "He is in the way of life that keeps instruction: but he that refuses reproof errs," Proverbs 10:17. It is the pious man that employs his mind upon the most proper and worthy objects, that knows things which of certainty are worthy to be known, "He that gets wisdom loves his own soul: he that keeps understanding shall find good," Proverbs 19:8. It is the pious man that has his soul enriched with the choicest notions, "The words of the wise are as goads, and as nails fastened by the masters of assemblies, which are given from one shepherd. And further, by these, my son, be admonished: of making many books there is no end; and much study is a weariness of the flesh. Let us hear the conclusion of the whole matter: Fear God, and keep his commandments: for this is the whole duty of man," Ecclesiastes 12:11-13. The pious man aims at the best ends and fits himself to attain them by the fittest means; he assigns to each thing its due worth and value;[1] he prosecutes a thing by the best method and orders his affairs in the best manner, so that he is sure not to be defeated or disappointed in his endeavors nor to waste his care and pains without answerable fruit therein. He has the best master to instruct him in his studies,[2] and the best

---

1. "The natural man receives not the things of the Spirit of God: for they are foolishness unto him: neither can he know them, because they are spiritually discerned. But he that is spiritual judges all things," 1 Corinthians 2:14-15.
2. "One is your Master, even Christ," Matthew 23:9-10, and, "You call me Master and Lord: and you say well; for so I am," John 13:13.

rules to direct him in his proceedings:[1] he cannot be mistaken, seeing in his judgment and choice of things he conspires with infallible wisdom.[2]

Therefore, ο ευσεβων αχρως φιλοσοφει, *the pious man is an exquisite philosopher*.[3] "The fear of the Lord, that is wisdom; and to depart from evil is understanding," Job 28:28. "The fear of the Lord is the beginning of wisdom: and the knowledge of the holy is understanding," Proverbs 9:10. "The fear of the Lord," as is said again and again in the Scriptures, "is the beginning of wisdom. A good understanding have all they that do his commandments," Psalms 111:10. "The fear of the Lord is the beginning of knowledge: but fools despise wisdom and instruction," Proverbs 1:7.[4]

---

1. Being "built upon the foundation of the Apostles and prophets, Jesus Christ himself being the chief corner stone," Ephesians 2:20-21; "Be mindful of the words which were spoken before by the holy prophets, and of the commandment of us the Apostles of the Lord and Savior," 2 Peter 3:2; and "All scripture is given by inspiration of God, and is profitable for doctrine, for reproof, for correction, for instruction in righteousness: that the man of God may be perfect, thoroughly furnished unto all good works," 2 Timothy 3:16-17.

2. "Thy testimonies also are my delight and my counsellors," Psalms 119:24. "The law of the Lord is perfect, converting the soul: the testimony of the Lord is sure, making wise the simple. The statutes of the Lord are right, rejoicing the heart: the commandment of the Lord is pure, enlightening the eyes," Psalms 19:7-8. Wisdom and understanding speak: "Counsel is mine, and sound wisdom: I am understanding; I have strength. By me kings reign, and princes decree justice. By me princes rule, and nobles, even all the judges of the earth," Proverbs 8:14-16.

3. Trismeg.

4. "Give me understanding, and I shall keep thy law; yea, I shall observe it with my whole heart," Psalms 119:34; "I have more understanding than all my teachers: for thy testimonies are my meditation," Psalms 119:99; "Through thy precepts I get

Further, the pious man is enabled and disposed—has the power and the heart—to benefit and oblige others most. He benefits others through his succor and assistance, through his instruction and advice, which he is ever ready to yield to any man upon fit occasion. He benefits others by the direction and encouragement of his good example. He benefits others by his constant and earnest prayers for all men. He benefits others by drawing down blessings from heaven on the place where he resides. He is upon all accounts the most true, the most common benefactor to mankind: all of his neighbors, his country, and the world are in some way or other obliged to him. He does all the good that he is able to, and he wishes a benefit upon all men.

Thus, all the fruits and consequences of profit, which do so engage men to very eagerly pursue it, do in the best kind and the highest degree result from piety, and indeed only from piety. All the philosophical bravadoes concerning a wise man being only rich, only honorable, only happy, only above fortune, are verified only in the pious man: to him alone, as being pious, with a sure foundation, without vanity, with evident reason, are those aphorisms applied. They are paradoxes and fictions removed from religion, or considering men only under the light and power of nature; but believing

---

understanding: therefore I hate every false way," Psalms 119:104; and "The entrance of thy words gives light; it gives understanding unto the simple," Psalms 119:130.

our religion to be true, a good Christian soberly, without arrogance, in proportion and according to the measure of his piety, may assume such axioms to himself, as the holy Apostles did: "I possess all things,"[1] and "I can do all things through Christ which strengthens me," Philippians 4:13, and so may the pious man also say after St. Paul.

As for all other kinds of profit, excluding that which is the fruit of piety, they are but imaginary and counterfeit, mere shadows and illusions, yielding only painted shows instead of substantial fruit.

If from bare worldly wealth—that which usurps the name of profit in this world—a man seeks honor, he is deluded, for he is not thereby truly honorable; he is but a shining earthworm, a well ornamented ass, a gaudy statue, a theatrical grandee.[2] With God, who judges most rightly, he is low and despicable: no intelligent person can inwardly respect him. Even here, in this world of deception and foolishness, the wisest and the most sober men, whose judgments usually sway others, cannot but contemn him, as master of no real good, nor fit for any good purpose; as seeing that, in the end he will prove most beggarly and wretched. "Because you say, I am rich, and increased with

---

1. "As unknown, and yet well known; as dying, and, behold, we live; as chastened, and not killed; as sorrowful, yet always rejoicing; as poor, yet making many rich; as having nothing, and yet possessing all things," 2 Corinthians 6:9-10.
2. Nobleman.

goods, and have need of nothing; and know not that you art wretched, and miserable, and poor, and blind, and naked: I counsel thee to buy of me gold tried in the fire, that thou may be rich; and white raiment, that thou may be clothed, and that the shame of thy nakedness do not appear; and anoint thine eyes with eyesalve, that thou may see," Revelation 3:17-18.

If a man affects power because he is rich and increased in many things, he is grievously mistaken: for, instead of power, he proves exceedingly feeble, and impotent, able to perform nothing worthy of a man, subject to foolish humors and passions, servant to diverse lusts and pleasures, captivated by the devil at his will,[1] overborne by temptation, hurried along by the currents of this world, and liable to every stroke of fortune.[2]

If he proposes to himself that the enjoyment of pleasure will be through riches and wealth, he will also much fail therein: for in lieu of riches and wealth he shall find care and trouble, surfeiting and disease, wearisome satiety and bitter regret; being

---

1. A reference to: "In meekness instructing those that oppose themselves; if God peradventure will give them repentance to the acknowledging of the truth; And that they may recover themselves out of the snare of the devil, who are taken captive by him at his will," 2 Timothy 2:25-26.
2. "It is not the man who has too little, but the man who craves more, that is poor. What does it matter how much a man has laid up in his strongbox or in his warehouse, how large are his flocks and how fat his dividends, if he covets his neighbor's property, and reckons, not his past gains, but his hopes of gains to come?" Seneca, *Moral Epistles, Ep. ii.*

void of all true delight in his mind and satisfaction in his conscience; nothing on this earth being able to furnish solid and stable pleasure. "Give me neither poverty nor riches; feed me with food convenient for me: lest I be full, and deny thee, and say, Who is the Lord? Or lest I be poor, and steal, and take the name of my God in vain," Proverbs 30:8-9.

If he imagines safety, he deludes himself, for how can he be safe, who is destitute of God's protection and succor; and how can he be safe who is the object of divine wrath and vengeance; who is assailed by many fierce and powerful enemies; whom the roaring lion is ready to devour; whom death and "sudden destruction" are coming to seize upon, "For yourselves know perfectly that the day of the Lord so comes as a thief in the night. For when they shall say, Peace and safety; then sudden destruction comes upon them, as travail upon a woman with child; and they shall not escape," 1 Thessalonians 5:2-3; whom guilt threatens and hell gapes for;[1] who without any defense stand exposed to such imminent, such horrid and ghastly dangers?[2]

If he thirsts for liberty, he will be frustrated, for he can be no other than a slave while he continues

---

1. "The way of the Lord is strength to the upright: but destruction shall be to the workers of iniquity," Proverbs 10:29.
2. "Woe to the rebellious children, says the Lord, that take counsel, but not of me; and that cover with a covering, but not of my Spirit," Isaiah 30:1.

impious: *servus tot dominorum, quot vitiorum,*[1] "a slave to as many masters as he keeps vices"—a slave to himself and his own lusts, carrying about with him the fetters of insatiable desire and being hampered by inconsistent and irregular affections.

Ease he cannot obtain, being oppressed with the unwieldy burdens of sin, of care, and of trouble; being tossed with restless agitations of lust and passion; being "like the troubled sea, which cannot rest, whose waters cast up mire and dirt," Isaiah 57:20.

If he means to get wisdom, he is at a loss, for wisdom and impiety are incompatible things. All his knowledge is vain, all his speculations are no better than dreams, seeing he errs in the main point and is not wise unto salvation: "The holy Scriptures," says the Apostle, "are able to make you wise unto salvation through faith which is in Christ Jesus. All scripture is given by inspiration of God, and is profitable for doctrine, for reproof, for correction, for instruction in righteousness: that the man of God may be perfect, thoroughly furnished unto all good works," 2 Timothy 3:15-17.

He is, in fine, extremely mistaken and in all his endeavors he will be lamentably disappointed, that is, whoever he is who imagines any true profit without piety. Such a man can never attain to be as wealthy as he who is supplied of the true and

---

1. Augustine.

real wealth of God's grace, in peace and in piety, but must drudge and plod what he can out of the feeble illusions and shadows of this world; he must continue a beggar and a forlorn wretch, "Knowest not that you art wretched, and miserable, and poor, and blind, and naked: I counsel thee to buy of me gold tried in the fire, that thou may be rich; and white raiment, that thou may be clothed," Revelation 3:17-18. How can he be in any way rich, who is lacking all the best things, the only things of value in this world, which any man may have and which any good man possesses?[1] How can he be rich, who is destitute of the most necessary accommodations of life: who constantly feeds on the coarsest and most sordid fare—the dust of pelf[2] and the dung of sensuality; who has no faithful or constant friends, nothing on this earth being a true and faithful friend; and who is master of nothing but dirt, chaff, and smoke? Whereas a great portion of the value of riches consists not in what one enjoys at present—which can be but little—but in the expectation of enjoyment later, with much ease, which hope may only come, through some stroke of bad fortune, to need; yet wealth holds out that which is believed to be a well-grounded hope that he who has it shall never fall into want or distress.

How can that man be rich, who has not any

---

1. "The sleep of a laboring man is sweet, whether he eat little or much: but the abundance of the rich will not suffer him to sleep," Ecclesiastes 5:12.
2. Money or wealth, in the sense of its lack of real value or gain.

confidence in God, any interest in God, or any reason to expect God's blessing? Yea, who has much reason to fear the displeasure of God, in whose hand are all things and who arbitrarily disposes of all things?

"Riches profit not in the day of wrath: but righteousness delivers from death," Proverbs 11:4. Piety therefore is the only profitable thing, according to just esteem: "Happy is the man that finds wisdom, and the man that gets understanding. For the merchandise of it is better than the merchandise of silver, and the gain thereof than fine gold. She is more precious than rubies: and all the things you can desire are not to be compared unto her. Length of days is in her right hand; and in her left hand riches and honor. Her ways are ways of pleasantness, and all her paths are peace. She is a tree of life to them that lay hold upon her: and happy is everyone that retains her," Proverbs 3:13-18. Upon this account it is most true, what the Psalmist affirms, "A little that the righteous has is better than great riches of the ungodly," Psalms 37:16.

IV.
Piety has the promise of the life that now is and of that which is to come.

That commendation is not to be omitted, which is nearest at hand and suggested by St. Paul himself, to support the assertion concerning the universal profitableness of piety; "For," says Paul, "godliness is profitable unto all things, having promise of the life that now is, and of that which is to come," 1 Timothy 4:8. That is, God has promised to reward godliness with blessings which appertain to this mortal life, and with those blessings which appertain to the future and eternal state.

As for the blessings of this life, although God has not promised to load the godly man with an abundance of worldly things; neither has God promised to put the godly man into splendid and pompous garb; neither has God promised to dispense to the godly man that which may serve for pampering the flesh or gratifying wanton desires; neither has God promised to exempt the godly man from all the inconveniences to which human nature and this worldly state are subject; yet God has promised to furnish the godly man with whatever is needful or convenient for him, in due measure and in due season, which things God does best understand. There is no good thing that a man naturally desires or reasonably can wish for, which is not in express terms proposed as a reward, or as a result of true piety.

Scriptural blessings upon the pious.

In general, it is declared by the Spirit in the Scriptures:

That "Blessings are upon the head of the just," Proverbs 10:6. "The Lord shall command the blessing upon thee in thy storehouses, and in all that thou settest thine hand unto; and he shall bless thee in the land which the Lord thy God gives thee," Deuteronomy 28:8. "And the Lord thy God will make thee plenteous in every work of thine hand, in the fruit of thy body, and in the fruit of thy cattle, and in the fruit of thy land, for good: for the Lord will again rejoice over thee for good, as he rejoiced over thy fathers," Deuteronomy 30:9.

That, "The Lord God is a sun and shield: the Lord will give grace and glory: no good thing will he withhold from them that walk uprightly," Psalms 84:11.

That, whatever otherwise falls out, "surely I know that it shall be well with them that fear God, which fear before him," Ecclesiastes 8:12. "Say ye to the righteous, that it shall be well with him: for they shall eat the fruit of their doings," Isaiah 3:10.

That, "Blessed is everyone that fears the Lord; that walks in his ways. For you shall eat the labor of your hands: happy shall you be, and it shall be well with you," Psalms 128:1-2. "For whoso finds me *(wisdom)* finds life, and shall obtain favor of the Lord," Proverbs 8:35.

That, "There shall no evil happen to the just," Proverbs 12:21.

That, "We know that all things work together for good to them that love God, to them who are the called according to his purpose," Romans 8:28.

Scriptural promises to the pious man.

Particularly, there are promised to the pious man in the Word of God:

A supply of all his wants: "The Lord will not suffer the soul of the righteous to famish," Proverbs 10:3. "The righteous eats to the satisfying of his soul," Proverbs 13:25. "Oh fear the Lord, ye his saints: for there is no want to them that fear him. The young lions do lack, and suffer hunger: but they that seek the Lord shall not want any good thing," Psalms 34:9-10.

A protection in all dangers: "Behold, the eye of the Lord is upon them that fear him, upon them that hope in his mercy; to deliver their soul from death, and to keep them alive in famine," Psalms 33:18-19. "They shall not be ashamed in the evil time: and in the days of famine they shall be satisfied," Psalms 37:19. "He shall not be afraid of evil tidings: his heart is fixed, trusting in the Lord," Psalms 112:7. "The Lord loves judgment, and forsakes not his saints; they are preserved forever," Psalms 37:28. "There shall no evil befall thee, neither shall any plague come near thy dwelling: he shall give his angels charge over thee, to keep thee in all thy ways," Psalms 91:10-11.

Guidance in all his undertakings and proceedings: "The steps of a good man are ordered by the Lord: and he delights in his way. Though he fall, he shall not be utterly cast down: for the

Lord upholds him with his hand," Psalms 37:23-24. "The law of his God is in his heart; none of his steps shall slide," Psalms 37:31. "In all thy ways acknowledge him, and he shall direct thy paths," Proverbs 3:6. "The integrity of the upright shall guide them. The righteousness of the perfect shall direct his way," Proverbs 11:3, 5. "Delight thyself also in the Lord; and he shall give thee the desires of thine heart," Psalms 37:4.

Success and prosperity in his designs: "Commit thy way unto the Lord; trust also in him; and he shall bring it to pass. And he shall bring forth thy righteousness as the light, and thy judgment as the noonday," Psalms 37:5-6. "He shall be like a tree planted by the rivers of water, that brings forth his fruit in his season; his leaf also shall not wither; and whatsoever he does shall prosper," Psalms 1:3. "Then shall thy light break forth as the morning, and thine health shall spring forth speedily: and thy righteousness shall go before thee; the glory of the Lord shall be thy rearward," Isaiah 58:8. "The Lord shall command the blessing upon thee in thy storehouses, and in all that thou settest thine hand unto," Deuteronomy 28:8. "The Lord shall open unto thee his good treasure, the heaven to give the rain unto thy land in his season, and to bless all the work of thine hand: and thou shalt lend unto many nations, and thou shalt not borrow," Deuteronomy 28:12. "Thine expectation shall not be cut off," Proverbs 23:18.

Comfortable enjoyment of the fruits of his industry: "Thou shalt eat the labor of thine hands: happy shalt thou be, and it shall be well with thee," Psalms 128:2.

Satisfaction of all reasonable desires: "The desire of the righteous shall be granted," Proverbs 10:24. "Delight thyself in the Lord, and he shall give thee the desires of thine heart," Psalms 37:4. "He will fulfill the desire of them that fear him: he will hear their cry, and will save them," Psalms 145:19.

Firm peace and quiet: "The work of righteousness shall be peace; and the effect of righteousness, quietness and assurance forever," Isaiah 32:17. "Great peace have they which love thy law: and nothing shall offend them," Psalms 119:165. "Behold the upright: for the end of that man is peace," Psalms 37:37. "The fruit of righteousness is sowed in peace," James 3:18.

Joy and cheerfulness: "Light is sown for the righteous, and gladness for the upright in heart," Psalms 97:11. "In the transgression of an evil man there is a snare: but the righteous sings and rejoices," Proverbs 29:6.

Support and comfort in afflictions: "He heals the broken in heart, and binds up their wounds," Psalms 147:3. "Be of good courage, and he shall strengthen your heart, all you that hope in the Lord," Psalms 31:24.

Deliverance from trouble: "Many are the afflictions of the righteous, but the Lord delivers him out of them all," Psalms 34:19. "But the salvation of the righteous is of the Lord: he is their strength in the time of trouble," Psalms 37:39.

Preservation and recovery from mishaps and miscarriages: "Though he fall, he shall not be utterly cast down: for the Lord upholds him with his hand," Psalms 37:24. "When I fall, I shall arise; when I sit in darkness, the Lord shall be a light unto me," Micah 7:8.

Preferment of all sorts, to honor and dignity, to wealth and prosperity: "Wait upon the Lord, and keep his way; and he shall exalt thee to inherit the land," Psalms 37:34. "By humility and fear of the Lord are riches and honor," Proverbs 22:4. "Blessed is the man that fears the Lord. Wealth and riches are in his house," Psalms 112:1, 3. "The upright shall have good things in possession," Proverbs 28:10. "If they obey and serve him, they shall spend their days in prosperity, and their years in pleasure," Job 36:11. "The tabernacle of the righteous shall flourish," Proverbs 14:11.

Long life: "The fear of the Lord prolongs days," Proverbs 10:27. "By me thy days shall be multiplied, and the years of thy life shall be increased," Proverbs 9:11. "Let thine heart keep my commandments: for length of days, and long life, and peace, shall they add unto thee," Proverbs 3:1-2.

A good name enduring after death: "The memory of the just is blessed," Proverbs 10:7. "He is ever merciful, and lendeth; and his seed is blessed," Psalms 37:26.

Blessings entailed on posterity: "His seed shall be mighty upon earth; the generation of the upright shall be blessed," Psalms 112:2. "The root of the righteous shall not be moved," Proverbs 12:3.

Thus is a liberal dispensation even of temporal goods enjoined by God's infallible Word upon the practice of piety. It is indeed more frequently, abundantly, and explicitly promised unto God's ancient people,[1] as being a conditional ingredient of the Covenant made by God with them, and exhibited in that covenant as a recompense of the external performance of the religious works that were prescribed in their Law. The Gospel does not so clearly propound temporal benefits, or so much insist upon them, as these are not

---

1. "The righteous shall be recompensed in the earth," Proverbs 11:31; "And it shall come to pass, if thou shalt hearken diligently unto the voice of the Lord thy God, to observe and to do all his commandments which I command thee this day, that the Lord thy God will set thee on high above all nations of the earth," Deuteronomy 28:1; "Wherefore it shall come to pass, if you hearken to these judgments, and keep, and do them, that the Lord thy God shall keep unto thee the covenant and the mercy which he sware unto thy fathers: and he will love thee, and bless thee, and multiply thee, etc.," Deuteronomy 7:12-13; and "It shall come to pass, if ye shall hearken diligently unto my commandments which I command you this day, to love the Lord your God, and to serve him with all your heart and with all your soul, that I will give you the rain of your land in his due season, the first rain and the latter rain, etc.," Deuteronomy 11:13-14.

principally belonging to the Evangelical Covenant, which Covenant, in regards to the performance of its conditions by us, peculiarly offers spiritual blessings, rather than temporal blessings, and relates to the future state. Neither do temporal benefits principally belong to the Evangelical Covenant, as scarcely deserving to be mentioned in comparison to those superior blessings of eternity: "For our light affliction, which is but for a moment, works for us a far more exceeding and eternal weight of glory," 2 Corinthians 4:17. And again, "For I reckon that the sufferings of this present time are not worthy to be compared with the glory which shall be revealed in us," Romans 8:18.

Yet, as the celestial benefits, although not openly given in the Jewish Law, were yet hidden therein in a mystery, designed for the spiritual and true practicers of religion, so also is the conferring of temporal accommodations to be understood to belong to all pious Christians. There is a codicil,[1] as it were, affixed to the New Testament, in which God signifies his intention to furnish his children with all that is needful or convenient for them. His providence has not ceased to watch over us, his bounty does not fail toward us even in this respect, his care will not be lacking to feed us and clothe us comfortably, to protect us from evil, and to prosper our good undertakings. Hence he commands us to "Be careful for nothing; but in everything by prayer and supplication with thanksgiving let your

---

1. A written supplement to a legal will.

requests be made known unto God," Philippians 4:6; to "cast our care upon him," 1 Peter 5:7; and to recommend our business to him, because he cares for us. "Let your conversation be without covetousness; and be content with such things as you have: for he hath said, I will never leave thee, nor forsake thee," Hebrews 13:5. "Take no thought for your life, what you shall eat, or what you shall drink; nor yet for your body, what you shall put on. Is not the life more than meat, and the body than raiment?" Matthew 6:25. He will hear our prayers, and help us. Hence we are enjoined "not to trust in uncertain riches, but in the living God, who gives us richly all things to enjoy," 1 Timothy 6:17. Hence it is said, that "The divine power has given us all things pertaining unto life and godliness, through the knowledge of him that has called us to glory and virtue," 2 Peter 1:3. Hence it is promised by our Lord, that, if we "seek first the kingdom of God, and his righteousness, all things shall be added to *(us)*," Matthew 6:33. Hence it is inferred, as consequential to the nature of the Evangelical dispensation, that we cannot lack any good thing. "He," says St. Paul, "that spared not his own Son, but delivered him up for us all, how shall he not with him also freely give us all things?" Romans 8:32.

In fine, it is thus proposed as evident that nothing is permitted to fall out other than what is conducive to our good. "We know," says St. Paul, "that all things work together for good unto those that love God," Romans 8:28. Nor will God, in any case, suffer us to be tempted by any lack or any pressure beyond what we are able to bear: "There has no temptation taken you but such as is common to man: but God is faithful, who will not suffer you to be tempted above that you are able; but will with the temptation also make a way to escape, that you may be able to bear it," 1 Corinthians 10:13.

Thus, piety is manifestly profitable, as "having promise of the life that now is," 1 Timothy 4:8— that is, as offering all temporal blessings that are, in the dispensation of God, desirable to those who practice piety in truth.

And infinitely more profitable is that sincere and true practice of piety, as having the promises of a future life, and as procuring a title to those incomparably more excellent blessings of the other world—for these are indefectible treasures; they are "an inheritance incorruptible, and undefiled, and that fades not away, reserved in heaven for you," 1 Peter 1:4; they are that exceeding weight of glory that is wrought for us, "For our light affliction, which is but for a moment, works for us a far more exceeding and eternal weight of glory," 2 Corinthians 4:17; they are those ineffable joys of paradise, "Yet believing," he says, "you rejoice with joy unspeakable and full of glory," 1 Peter 1:8, and "rejoice, inasmuch as you are partakers of Christ's sufferings; that, when his glory shall be revealed, you may be glad also with exceeding joy," 1 Peter

4:13; they are that illuminated countenance and beautifying presence of God, and that inconceivably and inexpressibly joyful, glorious, perfect, and endless bliss.

Briefly, the blessings that are promised to the true practice of piety are all that is intimated and contained in the words of the Apostle, "Eye has not seen, nor ear heard, neither have entered into the heart of man, the things which God has prepared for them that love him," 1 Corinthians 2:9.

That then is infinitely profitable that is able to secure all these things for us and, in looking to these, St. Paul had great reason to say that "Godliness is profitable unto all things," 1 Timothy 4:8.

GODLINESS
IS
PROFITABLE
FOR ALL THINGS

PART II

Advantages that arise
from the practice of piety

ADVANTAGES
THAT ARISE FROM THE
PRACTICE OF PIETY

"Godliness is profitable for all things."
1 Timothy 4:8

To further evidence and recommend this point, I would offer for consideration certain peculiar advantages arising from piety, which have a very general influence upon our lives, and afford us exceeding benefit. These more particular things will serve to confirm the assertion of St. Paul in relation to the profitability of godliness, being conducive to the same purpose and declaring the vast utility of religion or piety.

I.
Religion prescribes the truest and best rules of action.

We may consider, that religion prescribes the truest and best rules of action. It enlightens our minds and rectifies our practice in all matters and upon all occasions. Whatever then is performed according to true religion is done well and wisely, and he who practices it does all things with a comely grace in regard to others, with a cheerful satisfaction in his own mind, and with the best assurance—that things are in this world capable of producing—that he shall find a happy success and beneficial fruit in all he does.

The benefit of walking in the light.

Of all things in the world there is nothing more generally profitable than light: by it we are able to converse with the world and have all things set clearly before us; by it we truly and easily discern things in their right magnitude, shape, and color; by it we guide our steps safely in the accomplishing of what is good and in the shunning of what is noxious and harmful; by it our spirits are comfortably warmed and cheered, and our life consequently, our health, our strength, and our diligence in the daily pursuit of our business and interests are preserved.

The same benefits are yielded to us by true religion—which is the light of our soul.

Pious men are the "children of the light,"[1] Luke 16:8. "For you were sometimes darkness, but now are you light in the Lord: walk as children of light," Ephesians 5:8. "You are all the children of light, and the children of the day: we are not of

---

1. In the Greek, τους υιους του φωτος; and the Latin, *filiis lucis (Vulgate)*.

the night, nor of darkness," 1 Thessalonians 5:5. "Believe in the light, that you may be the children of light," John 12:36.

Pious works are works of light shining before men. "Let your light so shine before men, that they may see your good works, and glorify your Father which is in heaven," Matthew 5:16.[1]

God's Word—*or true religion*—is a lamp unto our feet, and a light unto our path: "How sweet are thy words unto my taste! Yea, sweeter than honey to my mouth! Through thy precepts I get understanding: therefore I hate every false way. Thy Word is a lamp unto my feet, and a light unto my path," Psalms 119:103-105.

God's Word—*or true religion*—enables us to perceive things and to judge them rightly. It teaches us to walk straightly and surely, without erring or stumbling. It qualifies us to embrace what is useful and to avoid what is hurtful, preserving our spiritual life and disposing us to act well with a ready willingness.

Without God's Word—*or true religion*—a man is stark blind and utterly overtaken by darkness. He must grope about in hesitation and doubt, "They have made them crooked paths: whosoever goes therein shall not know peace. Therefore is judgment far from us, neither does justice overtake

---

1. Conversely: "Have no fellowship with the unfruitful works of darkness, but rather reprove them," Ephesians 5:11.

us: we wait for light, but behold obscurity; for brightness, but we walk in darkness. We grope for the wall like the blind, and we grope as if we had no eyes: we stumble at noonday as in the night; we are in desolate places as dead men," Isaiah 59:8-10; he must wander in error, tripping upon all occasions and often falling into mischief, "If you will not hearken unto the voice of the Lord, the Lord shall smite you with madness, and blindness, and astonishment of heart: And you shall grope at noonday, as the blind gropes in darkness, and you shall not prosper in your ways: and you shall be only oppressed and spoiled evermore, and no man shall save you," Deuteronomy 28:15, 28-29. "The path of the just," says the wise Solomon, "is as the shining light. The way of the wicked is as darkness, they know not at what they stumble," Proverbs 4:18-19. "Righteousness keeps him that is upright in the way; but wickedness overthrows the sinner," Proverbs 13:6. "The integrity of the upright shall guide them: but the perverseness of transgressors shall destroy them. The righteousness of the perfect shall direct his way: but the wicked shall fall by his own wickedness," Proverbs 11:3, 5.[1]

---

1. "Let others be wise to their own destruction - let them establish their own imaginations for the Word of God and rule of their faith - but you hold fast what you have received and 'contend earnestly for it'. Add nothing, and diminish nothing; let this lamp shine 'till the day dawn,' 'till the morning of the resurrection,' and walk in the light of it and do not kindle any other sparkles, else you shall lie down in the grave in sorrow and rise in sorrow. Take the Word of God as the only rule, and the perfect rule - a rule for all your actions, civil, natural, and religious, for all must be done to his glory, and his Word teaches how to attain to that end. Let not your imaginations, let not others example, let not the preaching of men, let not the conclusions

The manifest benefits of a pious manner.

It is a fair adornment of a man and a great convenience both to himself and to all those with whom he converses and deals, to act uprightly, uniformly, and consistently. The practice of piety frees a man from interior distraction and from irresolution in his mind, from duplicity or inconstancy in his character, and from confusion in his proceedings, and consequently securing for others freedom from deception and disappointment in their transactions with him. Thus, some say, even a bad rule that is constantly observed is better than none: order and perseverance in any manner seems more convenient than roving about and tossing about in uncertainties.[1] But God's Word holds out the better and perfect rule, "That we henceforth be no more children, tossed to and fro, and carried about with every wind of doctrine, by the sleight of men, and cunning craftiness, whereby they lie in wait to deceive; but speaking the truth in love," Ephesians 4:14-15.

Excluding a regard for the precepts of true religion, there can hardly be any sure or settled rule, which can firmly engage a man to, or effectually restrain a man from, anything whatsoever.

There is scarcely in anything a nature that

and acts of Assemblies be your rule, but inasmuch as you find them agreeing with the perfect rule of God's Holy Word." Hugh Binning, *The Common Principles of the Christian Religion.*

1. *Via eunti aliquid extremum est; error immensus est.* Seneca, *Ep. xvi.*

is as wild, as intractable, or as unintelligible as a man who has no bridle of conscience to guide or restrain him. A profane man is like a ship without an anchor to stay him, or a rudder to steer him, or a compass to guide him, so that he is tossed with every wind and driven with every wave, no one knows where—wherever his fleshly temper sways him, or his passions hasten and drive him, or his interests pull him, or wherever the latest example that he observes leads him, wherever the latest company entices and draws him, or wherever the latest humor transports him. Indeed, wherever any such variable and unaccountable causes determine a direction and path for him or, when diverse causes together distract him so that he wanders and hesitates and can seldom himself tell in any case what he should do, nor can another guess what he will do, so that you cannot at any time know where to find him or how to deal with him, you cannot ever with reason rely upon him—so unstable is he in all his ways.[1] He is in effect a mere child, all humor and giddiness, and he is somewhat worse than a beast, which, following the instinct of its nature, is constant and consistent and thus is tractable or it is, according to its constant nature, so intractable that no man is deceived in meddling with him nor will he attempt it. Nothing therefore can be more unmanly than such a person; nothing

---

1. "A double minded man is unstable in all his ways," James 1:8.

can be more unpleasant than to have anything whatsoever to do with him.[1]

But a pious man, being steadily governed by conscience, and that conscience enlightened by the true religion of Godliness, regarding principles that are certain and sure, does both understand himself and is intelligible to others. The pious man presently sees what he is to do in every case, and can render an account of his actions. Such a man you may know candidly, and you may assuredly and reliably tell what he will do and thus, you may fully entrust a thing to his fidelity.

What law and government are to the public—things necessary to preserve the world in order, peace, and safety, that men may know what to do, and distinguish what is their own—the same is piety as it governs each man's private state and all ordinary conversation. Piety, by rule and justice, frees a man's life from disorder and distraction. It prompts men and guides them in how to behave themselves toward one another with security and confidence.

Piety is able to do this by confining our practice within the settled bounds of godliness. The advantage of this is greater than it appears, considering that the rules which piety prescribes are the best that can be. And such they must

---

1. *Nihil est tam occupatum, tam multiforme, tot ac tam variis affectibus concisum atque laceratum, quam mala mens.* Quint., xii. 1.

necessarily be, as they proceed from infallible wisdom and immense goodness. Indeed, being no other than the laws of the all-wise and most gracious Lord and Maker of the world, who, out of tender kindness toward us who were created by him and are subject to him, has been pleased to enact and declare according to his own principal regard for our welfare. What God said of old to the people of Israel concerning their laws, may with greater advantage be applied to those laws that should regulate our lives: "And now, Israel, what does the Lord your God require of you, but to fear the Lord your God, to walk in all his ways, and to love him, and to serve the Lord your God with all your heart, and with all your soul; to keep the commandments of the Lord, and his statutes, which I command you this day for your good?" Deuteronomy 10:12-13.

"For your good"—that was the design of their being commanded, and the observance of them did tend and contribute to the good of the people of Israel. And this is the commendation that was given to that law by the Levites in Nehemiah, but which commendation more plainly and fully agrees with the Christian institution, general and perfect: "You came down also upon mount Sinai, and spoke with them from heaven, and gave them right judgments, and true laws, good statutes and commandments," Nehemiah 9:13.

"The law," says the Apostle Paul, "is holy; the

commandment is holy, just, and good," Romans 7:12. As such—as being holy, just, and good—it is recommended to us by God, its Author, so that we, particularly we who are Christians, are by many great arguments assured that it is. But that the law is holy, just, and good even natural reason dictates. So also, as to the chief instances of that law, the most wise and sober men have always acknowledged, so also the general consent avows, and so also, even common experience attests. For, heartily to love and reverence the Creator of all things—who demonstrates by every apparent[1] before us, by all things seen, that he is incomprehensibly powerful, wise, and good[2]—and to be kind and charitable to our neighbors, to be just and faithful in our dealings, to be sober and modest in our minds, to be meek and gentle in our demeanor, to be moderate and temperate in our enjoyments, and the like principal rules of duty, are such that common reason among men and continual experience approves them as hugely conducive to the public good of men and to each man's private welfare.

So manifestly beneficial do the holy

---

1. All those things that can be seen: "That which may be known of God is manifest in them; for God hath shewed it unto them. For the invisible things of him from the creation of the world are clearly seen, being understood by the things that are made, even his eternal power and Godhead; so that they are without excuse: Because that, when they knew God, they glorified him not as God, neither were thankful; but became vain in their imaginations, and their foolish heart was darkened," Romans 1:19-21.
2. "Great is our Lord, and of great power: his understanding is infinite," Psalms 147:5.

commandments of God appear that for the justification of them we might appeal even to the judgment and conscience of those persons who are most concerned with the derogation of them. For hardly can any man be so senseless or so lewd, as seriously to disapprove or condemn them, or as inwardly to blame or slight those who truly act according to them. The will of men sometimes may be so depraved that dissolute persons wantonly and heedlessly scoff at and seem to disparage goodness, and good men are, for well-doing, envied and hated by very evil men—but their being so treated is commonly an argument of the goodness of their persons and of their ways.[1] The understanding of men, however, can hardly be so corrupt that piety, charity, justice, temperance, and meekness can in good earnest or with consideration be disallowed or persons apparently practicing such things be despised. But, in spite of all contrary prejudices and disaffections, such things and such persons cannot but in judgment and heart be esteemed by all men. By a natural and necessary efficacy, the luster of them, like that of heaven's glorious light, dazzles the sight and charms the spirits of all living men; the beauty of them irresistibly conquers and commands in the apprehensions of men. The more such things as piety, charity, and justice are observed, the more useful and needful they appear for the good of all men, and the fruits which grow from the observance of them are to all men's taste

---

1. "The world," Jesus said, "hateth *(me)*, because I testify of it, that the works thereof are evil," John 7:7.

very pleasant and to all men's experience very wholesome.

Indeed, all the good by which common life is adorned, sweetened, and rendered pleasant and desirable, springs from the observance of piety, charity, and justice. And all the harm and injury that infests particular men and disturbs the world, palpably arises from the transgression or neglect of the practice of piety, charity, and justice. If we look on a person who sticks himself to those rules, we shall observe a man in whom is a cheerful mind and composed passions, who is at peace within, and satisfied with himself, whose life is in proper order, himself in good repute, in fair correspondence with good men and firm concord with his neighbors.

If we mark what preserves the body sound and healthy, what keeps the mind vigorous and brisk, what saves and improves an estate, what upholds a good name, what guards and graces a man's whole life, it is nothing else but the practice in our demeanor and in all our dealings, of the honest and wise rules of piety. If we see some place or locale where these rules are commonly and in good measure observed, we shall also discover that peace and prosperity flourish there; that all things proceed sweetly and fairly there; that men generally carry on conversation and commerce together contentedly, delightfully, and advantageously there, yielding friendly advice and aid mutually, striving to render one another happy. We shall discover that few clamors or complaints are heard there, few contentions or disturbances appear there, few disasters or tragedies occur there; indeed, that such a place has much of the appearance and much of the substance of Paradise.

But if you mind a person who neglects the practice of piety, charity, and justice, you will find his mind disturbed and injured with sore remorse, racked with anxious fears and doubts, agitated with storms of passion and lust, living in disorder and disgrace, jarring[1] with others, and no less dissatisfied with himself. If you observe what impairs the health, weakens and distresses the mind, wastes the estate, blemishes the reputation, exposes the whole life to danger and trouble, what is it but the thwarting and contravening of these good rules? If you consider a place where the practice of piety, charity, and justice are much neglected, it will appear like a wilderness of savage beasts, or a sty of foul swine, or a hell of cursed fiends. It will be full of roaring and tearing, of factions and feuds, of distractions and confusions, of pitiful objects, of doleful moans, and of tragic events. There men will be found wallowing in filth, reveling wildly, bickering and squabbling, defaming one another, circumventing, disturbing and vexing one another, even as if they hoped to achieve nothing more than to render one another as miserable as they can. It is from lust and luxury, from ambition and avarice, from envy and spite, and the like dispositions,

---

1. Discordant.

which religion chiefly interdicts and prohibits, that all such horrid injuries and ill consequences spring.

In fine, the precepts of religion are no other than such as physicians prescribe for the health of our bodies, as politicians avow to be needful for the peace of the state, as philosophers recommend for the tranquility of our minds and pleasantness of our lives. The precepts of true religion are such as common reason dictates and daily experience shows to be conducive to our welfare in all respects. Consequently, were there no law exacting these things of us, we should in wisdom choose to observe them and voluntarily impose them upon ourselves, confessing them to be the fittest matters of law and the most advantageous and requisite to the general and particular good of mankind. So that what Plutarch reported Solon to have said regarding the civil laws, that "he had so squared his laws to the citizens, that all of them might clearly perceive, that to observe them was more for their benefit and interest than to violate them,"[1] is far more true regarding the divine laws.

II.
The interior fruits of the practice of piety.

We may consider more particularly, that piety yields to the practicer of it every kind of interior contentment, peace, and joy, and frees him from every kind of dissatisfaction, regret, and disquiet,

---

1. Plutarch *in. Sol.*

which is an inestimably great advantage. For certain, the happiness and misery of men are wholly or chiefly seated and founded in the mind. If that is in a good state of health, rest, and cheerfulness, whatever the person's outward condition or circumstances may be, he cannot be wretched or anxious or sunk in affliction or distress; and if the state of the mind is disordered or disturbed, he cannot be happy. For what is it if a man seems very poor to others, if he is abundantly satisfied in his own possessions and enjoyments? What is it if a man partakes not of the pleasures of the senses, if he enjoys the purer and sweeter delights of the mind? What is it if tempests of fortune surround him, if his mind is calm and serene? What is it if a man has few or no friends, if he is yet thoroughly at peace and amity with himself, and can delightfully converse with his own thoughts? What is it if men slight, censure, or revile him, if he values his own state, approves his own actions, and acquits himself of blame in his own conscience according to right and true religion?

Such external contingencies can no more prejudice a man's real happiness, than winds blustering abroad can harm or trouble the man that abides in a safe place within doors, or than the storms and fluctuations of the waves at sea can trouble and disturb that man who stands firm upon the shore. "Thou wilt keep him in perfect peace, whose mind is stayed on thee: because he trusts in thee," Isaiah 26:3.

On the other hand, the greatest abundance of all those things that seem good will avail nothing if real contentment of mind is lacking. What will the highest eminence of outward state import to him that is dejected in his own opinion? What if the world courts and blesses him or if all people admire and applaud him, if he is displeased within, if he condemns himself, or if he despises himself? What if the weather looks fair and bright outside, if storms rage in his breast and if black clouds darken his soul? What if he abounds with friends and enjoys peace abroad, if he finds distraction at home and is at cruel variance with himself? How can a man enjoy any satisfaction or relish any pleasure, while sore remorse stings him or anxious doubts and fears rack him? "For," says Chrysostom, "as for good spirits and joy, it is not greatness of power, not abundance of wealth, not pomp of authority, not strength of body, not sumptuousness of the table, not the adorning of dresses, nor any other of the things in man's reach that ordinarily produces them, but spiritual success, and a good conscience alone. And he that has this cleansed, even though he be clad in rags and struggling with famine, is of better spirits than they that live so softly. So too he that is conscious of wicked deeds, even though he may gather to himself all men's goods, is the most wretched of all men."[1]

Now that from the practice of religion and

---

1. Chrysostom, *On the Epistle to the Romans*, Homily I. *(An enlarged passage from Chrysostom is included in Part III.)*

from it alone does such inward contentment and pleasure spring: true religion alone ministers reason for contentment and disposes the mind to enjoy it; it alone extirpates the grounds and roots of discontentment; it alone generates true and sober cheerfulness and tranquility of mind, which things all, upon consideration, will be made manifest.

There is no other thing here in this world that can yield any solid or stable contentment to our mind, for all present enjoyments are transient and vanishing away: "wealth is not forever, nor the crown from generation to generation," Proverbs 27:24.[1] And in this realm of change and contingency there can be no assurance of any future thing, "The race is not to the swift, nor the battle to the strong, neither yet bread to the wise, nor yet riches to men of understanding, nor yet favor to men of skill; but time and chance happens to them all," Ecclesiastes 9:11. There is nothing below, upon this earth, that is large enough to fill our vast capacities or to satiate our boundless desires or to appease our delicate tastes, "The eye is not satisfied with seeing, nor the ear filled with hearing," Ecclesiastes 1:8; "The eyes of man are never satisfied," Proverbs 27:20. Neither is there any sweet thing that we do not quickly drain off and exhaust or which we do not soon grow weary of or begin to consider quite loathsome or only faintly pleasing to us. There is nothing that is not slippery and fleeting so that we

---

1. "For what is your life? It is even a vapor, that appears for a little time, and then vanishes away," James 4:14.

could hope to possess it for a long time or enjoy it for any amount of time without restless care in keeping it and anxious fear of losing it. There is nothing that in the pursuance, the custody, the defense and maintenance of it we are not liable to disappointments, trials, and misfortunes.

Consequently there is nothing that produces any sound contentment in the disdainful, impatient, greedy, and restless heart of man. The greatest overflow of present, corporeal, and worldly things— of all the health, the riches, the dignity, the power, the friendships and dependencies, the learning and wisdom, the wit, or the reputation and renown in this world—will not afford much contentment. But this is only an imaginary supposition for, effectively, all such accommodations of life hardly unite in any state. There is always some dead fly in the ointment that mars our enjoyment or contentment; some inherent inconvenience that sours the gratification of our enjoyments. There is ever some good thing absent that we want or long for, and some ill thing present or in prospect, which we abhor and would avoid, fearing that it may come.

If, therefore, we would find contentment, we must not seek it here of this present world, but must want it and have it from another world—it must come here from heaven, and from heaven alone can piety draw it down upon us. Godliness, instead of these unsatisfying, uncertain, and unstable things, supplies us with goods adequate to our most far reaching wishes; it is infallibly sure, and incessantly durable; it is an indefectible treasure, an incorruptible inheritance, an unshakable kingdom, a perfect and endless joy, capable of replenishing the emptiest heart, which, he that has a good title to and a confident hope of, how can he be other than extremely pleased, than fully content? Godliness assures us of the favor and friendship of God—of God that is absolute Lord and disposer of all things—the favor and friendship of which he that has it and trusts therein, what can he want or wish more? What can he fear? What can annoy or dismay him? What can happen to him by chance or fortune that is worthy to be deemed evil or sad? What is poverty to him for whom God is concerned to provide and care for? What is disgrace to him who has the regard and approbation of God? What is danger to him, whom God continually protects? What can any distress work on him, whom God comforts and will relieve? What is anything to him, who is sensible that all things are purposely bestowed upon him by the perfect wisdom of God who knows what is best, and by the goodness of God, who entirely loves him?

In fine, he that is conscious in himself of being well-affected in mind and who conducts himself in the most upright way, who is satisfied in the state of his soul, secure from God's displeasure, and hopeful of his favor, what can make any grievous impression on him? What affections other than such as are most grateful and pleasant can lodge in his soul? Joy and peace have natural seeds in such a mind, and necessarily must spring up there, in proportion, I mean, and according to the degree of piety resident within that heart.

The Epicureans did imagine and boast that having, by their atheistic interpretations of natural effects and common events, discarded the belief and dread of religion, and had thus laid a strong foundation for tranquility of mind, having driven away all the causes of grief and fear so that there remained then nothing troublesome or terrible to men. Consequently, they said, what could prohibit men from being entirely contented, glad, and happy? *Nos exaequat victoria coelo,* no god then surely could be more happy than we. But, in many respects, their attempt was lame and vain. They presumed and believed in a victory which is impossible to obtain, and supposing they had obtained it, their triumph would not have been so glorious nor their success as great as they pretended. For seeing no Epicurean discourse can baffle the potent arguments which persuade men in favor of religion—that is, those arguments that the visible frame and structure of nature, the popular tradition of every age, the general consent of all men, and the pregnant attestations of history and experience concerning supernatural and miraculous events, do afford—since the very existence and the providence of God have proofs so clear and valid that no subtlety of man can so far evade them as not to be shaken by them or to be utterly freed from doubt and suspicion regarding their truth; and since there can be no means of evincing the negative part in those questions or demonstrating the negative to be true or even probable, it is impossible that any thinking and considering man, in this cause against religion, should suppose himself to have acquired a secure and absolute victory, or that he should reap substantial fruit of comfort from such. Neither is it possible that any man should enjoy any kind of perfect quiet without undertaking to obtain some good hope of avoiding those dreadful consequences that religion threatens upon the transgressors of its precepts.

Indeed, if there were only reason enough to stir an unbeliever, much less to cause an unbeliever to waver, or if it were somewhat doubtful whether there are punishments reserved, yea, if the odds were great that there are no punishments reserved for the ungodly—as indeed there *are* punishments reserved and the most perfect assurances imaginable of such punishments—yet, there is great advantage on the contrary side and wisdom itself would require that men should choose to be pious, since without piety in private and in common actions no man can be thoroughly secure.

Indeed, if there were *any* reason, even the smallest, to believe that judgment is to come—as there *are* manifestly very many and great reasons; and if most men concurred in the denial of Providence—as the commonality of mankind have ever generally consented together in avowing it; yet, even then, wisdom would require that men should choose to be pious, since otherwise no man can be thoroughly secure.

Indeed, if there were any pretence of miracles for establishing the doctrines of the mortality of the soul or the impunity of the soul—as there have been numerous miracles with the strong testimony of good witnesses and great events to confirm the opposite doctrines of the immortal nature of the soul and its culpability; and if the most wise and sober men judged in favor of irreligion—as commonly as they ever did and still do judge in favor of true religion; yet, even then, wisdom would require that men should choose to be pious, since otherwise no man can be thoroughly secure.

It is the disordering of all things not to dread the least possibility of incurring such horrible consequences, when so great a peril or any hazard of such importance should startle a man out of his wits.

To be in the least bit liable or subject to eternal torments, if men would think upon these things as men, that is, as rational and provident creatures, they could not but be disturbed by them. And indeed so it is in experience, for whatever they may say or whatever they may seem to be, all atheists and profane men are inwardly suspicious and fearful: they do not care to die and would gladly escape the trial of what shall follow death.[1] But let us grant or imagine the Epicurean or the atheist to be as successful as he could wish in this enterprise of subduing the truths and realities of religion, yet, except that he can also trample down reason and cast human nature in a new mold that he might subjugate all natural appetites and passions, and thus alter the state of things here in this world, indeed, and transform the world itself, yet he will in the greater part fall short of the advantages that he has imagined and he will fall very short of triumphing in a contented and quiet mind. That which will accrue to him will be at most no more than some negation that would appear to be contentment, or some portion of indolence arising from his being rescued or relieved from some particular cares and fears—which things do not exceed or are not better than the tranquility of a beast or the stupidity of one who is senseless. And that is all he can claim and yet, it is more than he can ever actually achieve, for he cannot be as a beast or a mere sot, even if he would. Reason, reflecting on present evils and foreboding future misfortunes, will afflict him, and his own insatiable desires, untamable passions, and unavoidable fears will disquiet him. Though the other world were by

---

1. "It must be so—Plato thou reasonest well. Else whence this pleasing hope, this fond desire, this longing after immortality? Or whence this secret dread, and inward horror, of falling into naught? Why shrinks the soul back on herself, and startles at destruction? Tis the divinity that stirs within us; tis heaven itself that points out an hereafter, and intimates eternity to man. Eternity, you pleasing, dreadful thought!" Joseph Addison, *Cato*, Act v. Sc. 1, 1713.

probable evidences discredited and unworthy of his faith, and thus placed quite out of his thoughts, yet this world by itself, yields sufficient enough trouble to render him unable to maintain any steady rest or solid joy.

The generality of men have always and always will complain that the burdens, crosses, and satieties[1] of this life far surpass the conveniences and comforts of it. So that, were there no other life to be expected or feared, this life of itself would become grievous and nauseating, *Non tempestate vexor, sed nausea.*[2] We should soon have enough or too much of it, without the support and a supply of rest and joy from elsewhere. Even in the greatest overflow of pleasant and refreshing things, and even in the deepest calmness of our state here, we are apt to begin to loath and become weary of even prosperity itself. Neither serenity nor abundance in this world are without ingredients not only somewhat unsavory, but very bitter and loathsome.

We may add that, had the profane philosophers not only attempted but quite banished religion, with it they would have driven away all the benefits and comforts of religion, which, even supposing such comforts to be no more than imaginary, are yet the greatest comforts which ordinary life needs or even can desire. And, had such men succeeded,

---

1. The excesses of pleasure or consumption that produces a weariness or disdain for a thing: "The full soul loathes an honeycomb," Proverbs 27:7.
2. Seneca, *de Tranq.* An. 1.

with the banishment of religion, they would have sent justice, fidelity, charity, sobriety, and all solid virtue packing—things which cannot firmly subsist without piety and uprightness of conscience, and which, being absent or banished with the true religion that produces them, human life would be rendered and become entirely disorderly and entirely unsafe, and thus the most wretched and contemptible thing that can be. What would then remain? Nothing but destitute and tasteless and flashy sensualities. These alone would remain to comfort a man and fill him, and they would hardly do so by reason of the lawless competitions and unrestrainable contentions that would ensue for them, which would allow no man to enjoy them quietly or safely.

It is piety alone, by raising the hope of blessings and joys incomparably superior to any that may be hoped for here and that cannot be taken from any man, which can lay any ground of true contentment and of such a substantial and positive contentment as consists not only in removing the objects and causes of vexatious passions, but in employing the most pleasant affections—love, hope, joy— with delightful satisfaction upon their proper and most noble objects. The kingdom of God and that only, with no other kingdom in the world having that privilege, consists in righteousness, and righteousness first, then in peace and spiritual joy.[1]

---

1. "For the kingdom of God is *(in)* righteousness, and peace, and joy in the Holy Spirit," Romans 14:17.

No philosopher can, within reason and truth, make that overture to us that our Lord does: "Come unto me, all you that are weary and heavy laden, and you shall find rest to your souls." Matthew 11:28-29. Outside of true religion there can be no such principle pretended like to that of the prophet, "Thou shall keep him in perfect peace, whose mind is stayed on thee," Isaiah 26:3.

If, indeed, we distinctly survey all the grounds and sources of contentment, it will appear that religion alone can afford it.

Does contentment result from the well ordering and governing of our passions? Then, it is plain, that only a pious man is capable thereof, for piety alone can effect this, it alone, through the powerful aid of divine grace, guides our passions by exact rules, sets them upon worthy objects, tempers and tunes them in proper harmony, seasonably curbs and restrains them, and rightly corrects and reforms them.[1]

This, no bare reason, which naturally is so dim and so feeble in man, can achieve—much less can unreasonableness achieve it, which unreasonableness is ever prevalent in irreligious persons. Their passions ever run wildly and at random, at no good pace, in no good direction, and toward the meanest and basest objects, wherein they can have no rest or quietness of mind. As

---

1. *Mala mens—cum insidiatur, spe, curis, labore distringitur; et jam cum sceleris compos fuerit, solicitudine, poenitentia, poenarum, omnium expectatione torquetur.* Quint., xii, 1.

they are constantly offending, so will they ever be punishing themselves with unrest, conflicts, and with dissatisfactions and regrets. Hence, "There is no peace, saith the Lord, unto the wicked," Isaiah 48:22. The ungodly "are like the troubled sea, when it cannot rest, whose waters cast up mire and dirt," Isaiah 57:20. "God," as St. Augustine says, "has said it, and so it is, every inordinate mind is a punishment to itself."[1]

Does contentment in a man spring from a hearty approbation of or satisfaction with a man's own actions, and from reflection that he constantly acts according to reason and wisdom, to justice and duty? Then can the pious man alone put in a claim to it, who knows that he walks inoffensively toward God and man, that he consults his own best interest and welfare, that assuredly no bad consequence can attend his unblamable behavior; that most wise men have declared their approbation of his proceedings; and, that if he were to be proven to have been mistaken in his chief design, yet no mischief will thereupon befall him, yea, that neither would he be even disappointed, seeing that much present satisfaction and convenience have sprung up from his practices.

Does contentment grow from a sound and healthy constitution of soul? It is the pious man alone that has this, for his mind is clear from the

---

1. *Deus jussit, et ita est, Sibi poena est omnis inordinatus animus.* Augustine, *Confessions.*

predominance of vice and passion. The impious man is infirm, disordered, and full of disturbances and pain,[1] according to the prophet's description of him: "The whole head is sick, and the whole heart faint. From the sole of the foot even unto the head there is no soundness in it; but wounds, and bruises, and putrefying sores: they have not been closed, neither bound up, neither mollified with ointment," Isaiah 1:5-6.

Does contentment arise particularly from good success in our attempts and from prosperous events befalling us? Then it is the pious man who is most capable of satisfaction of mind, for he alone is free from danger, and that which seems good and prosperous is really so to him, as all things are according to the divine goodness meant for his good and are directed toward his good by the guidance of God's infallible wisdom. As he alone has ground to hope for success because he confides in God, because he dutifully seeks God's help, because God is favorably disposed toward him, because God orders his steps, because God is pledged to bless him according to his promise, and because he is conscious of intentions to render God thanks and praise for it, to employ his success to God's honor and service, so the godly man alone can be satisfied with the appearance of success, being able with assurance to say after St. Paul that

---

1. The sense is biblical, as those who, coveting after riches, "pierced themselves through with many sorrows," or literally, "pains," (1 Timothy 6:10).

"We know that all things work together for good to them that love God," Romans 8:28.

Is security from danger, from trouble, from want, from all evil, a source or matter of contentment? It certainly does attend the pious man: God being his principal protector, his comforter, his provider. "There shall no evil befall the just," Proverbs 12:21; "There shall no plague come near his dwelling," Psalms 91:10. "The righteous cry, and the Lord hears, and delivers them out of all their troubles," Psalms 34:17. "The desire of the righteous shall be granted," Proverbs 10:24. "There is no want to them that fear God," Psalms 34:9. So do the Holy Scriptures assure us.

Does contentedness spring from sufficiency, real or imagined? This appertains peculiarly to the pious man, for, having God, the master of all, for his portion, he has the richest estate that can be; he has all that he can desire, he cannot but take himself to have enough. Hence, "Godliness with contentedness (μετ αυταρχειας, *with sufficiency*) is," as St. Paul says, "great gain," μεγας πορισμος, *the great way of gaining*, 1 Timothy 6:6.

He does not say this as if he supposed godliness and contentment were separable, but rather, as implying that godliness is great gain because sufficiency and contentment do always attend it.

In fine, if that saying of Seneca is true that, *Si cui sua non videntur amplissima, licet totius mundi dominus sit, tamen miser est*, "If to any man the things he possesses do not seem most ample, although he be master of the whole world, yet he would be miserable,"[1] then assuredly the pious man alone can be happy, for to him alone his possessions can seem the largest and best, such as there can be no possible accession[2] to or amendment of, for nothing can be better or greater than God, in whom he has a steadfast propriety,[3] whose infinite power and wisdom are engaged to do him the utmost good that he is capable of.

And further,

III.
Piety confers happiness.

Seeing that I have mentioned happiness, or the *summum bonum*, the utmost scope of human desire, I add, that piety does surely confer it. Happiness, whatever it may be, certainly has an essential coherence with piety. These are reciprocal propositions and both of them are infallibly true: he that is pious is happy and he that is happy is pious.

No man undertakes or pursues anything that he does not apprehend in some degree conducive to his own happiness, even that very happiness which all men under a confused notion regard and seek

---

1. Seneca, *Ep. ix.*
2. Increase.
3. A peculiar or exclusive right of possession.

as the highest good and the most desirable thing. But in their judgments about this thing and of the means of attaining it, as men dissent much one with another, thus, of necessity most of them must be mistaken in both regards. Indeed, most men aim and shoot at a mere shadow of profit, or at that which is in consideration, very little and in comparison nothing at all, which is hardly conducive to the perfection of their nature or the satisfaction of their desire. If they miss the mark, they are disappointed and if they hit it, they are no less disappointed, as if, in effect, they had gained nothing. But whatever this grand matter of happiness is, in whatever it consists and however it may be procured—be it the possession and fruition of some special choice goods, or the collection and over abundance of all goods—piety surely is the main ingredient and principal cause thereof. All other goods without piety are insignificant and useless to the happiness of men, yet happiness is not and cannot be lacking where piety is.

Though a man be ever so rich, so powerful, so learned and knowing, so prosperous in his affairs, so honorable in the opinions and affections of men, yet he can be in nowise happy if he is not pious. Without piety or godliness that man lacks the best goods and is subject to the worst evils— he lacks the love and favor of God, he lacks peace and satisfaction of conscience, he lacks a right enjoyment of present things, and he lacks security concerning his final welfare. And conversely, be a man ever so poor, so low in the eyes of men, so forlorn and destitute of worldly conveniences, yet if he is pious, he cannot be wretched, for he has an interest in goods incomparably precious and is safe from all considerable evils; he has and may freely resort to the inexhaustible fountain of all happiness, he has a right to immense and endless felicity, which encompasses in the highest degree all the good that we are capable of enjoying and intended to receive; he is possessed thereof in hope and certain reversion,[1] there is but a moment to pass before his complete fruition of it.

The lack of all other petty things can no more maim the integrity of his felicity, than cutting the hair or paring the nails, mutilates the man: all other things are but superfluities or overabundances in regard to the constitution of happiness. Whatever happens, that will assuredly be true which is so often inculcated in Holy Scripture, "Blessed is everyone that fears the Lord that walks in his ways. For you shall eat the labor of your hands: happy shall you be, and it shall be well with you," Psalms 128:1-2. "Praise ye the Lord. Blessed is the man that fears the Lord, that delights greatly in his commandments," Psalms 112:1.

Piety is indeed laden with beatitudes—every part thereof yields peculiar blessedness: to the love of God, to charity toward our neighbor, to purity of heart, to meekness, to humility, to patience, to

---

1. The right to future possession and enjoyment.

mercifulness, and to peaceableness. Blessedness is ascribed to it by our Lord, the great judge and dispenser of that blessedness. Each religious performance has happy fruits growing from it and blissful rewards assigned thereto. All pious dispositions are fountains of pleasant streams, which by their confluence do make up a full sea of felicity: "Blessed are the poor in spirit: for theirs is the kingdom of heaven. Blessed are they that mourn: for they shall be comforted. Blessed are the meek: for they shall inherit the earth. Blessed are they which do hunger and thirst after righteousness: for they shall be filled. Blessed are the merciful: for they shall obtain mercy. Blessed are the pure in heart: for they shall see God. Blessed are the peacemakers: for they shall be called the children of God. Blessed are they which are persecuted for righteousness' sake: for theirs is the kingdom of heaven. Blessed are you, when men shall revile you, and persecute you, and shall say all manner of evil against you falsely, for my sake," Matthew 5:3-11.

IV.
Piety furnishes employment suited and beneficial to us.

It is a peculiar advantage of piety that it furnishes employment fit for us, worthy of us, hugely gratifying, and highly beneficial to us. Man is a very busy and active creature—he cannot live and do nothing—whose thoughts are in restless motion, whose desires are ever exerted toward something, who perpetually will be working either good or evil for himself. Greatly profitable, therefore, must that thing be that determined that he should act well, to spend his care and pain on that which is truly advantageous to him—and that is religion alone. It alone fastens our thoughts, affections, and endeavors upon occupations worthy of the dignity of our nature, suited to the excellence of our natural capacities and endowments, and tending to the perfection and advancement of our reason, and to the enriching and ennobling of our souls. Excluding that, we have nothing in the world to study, to aspire to, or to pursue that is not of little estimation and below us, or very base and unbecoming to us as men of reason and judgment.

What have we to do but to eat and drink, like horses or like swine; or to sport and play, like children or apes; or to bicker and scuffle about trifles and impertinences, like idiots? What have we to do but to scrape or scramble for useless riches; to hunt after empty shows and shadows of honor, or the vain fancies and dreams of men?[1] What have we to do but to wallow or bask in sordid pleasures, which pleasures soon degenerate into remorse and

---

1. "Will you still be cheated by this deceitful world, and spend all your days in pampering your guts, and providing for the flesh, that must be rotting shortly in a grave? Were you made for no better use than this? May not we bring you to some sober thoughts of your condition? Not one hour seriously to think whither you are going? What! Not one awakened look into the world where you must be forever?" Rev. Richard Baxter, Preface to *An Alarm to Unconverted Sinners* by Rev. Joseph Alleine.

bitterness? To which sorts of employment, if a man were confined, what a pitiful thing would he be and how inconsiderable would his life become! Were a man designed like a fly only to buzz about here for a time, sucking in the air and licking the dew, then soon to vanish back into nothing or to be transformed into worms, how sorry and despicable a thing would he be?—And such, without religion, would we be.

But religion, that is, the true religion of God's Word, supplies us with business of a most worthy nature and lofty importance: it sets us upon doing things as great and noble as can be; it engages us to free our minds from all fond, self-flattering and vain conceits, and cleanse our hearts from all corrupt affections; to curb our brutish appetites, to tame our wild passions, to correct our perverse inclinations, to conform the dispositions of our soul and the actions of our life to the eternal laws of righteousness and goodness.[1] True religion sets us upon the imitation of God and aiming at the resemblance of his perfections;[2] upon obtaining a friendship and maintaining a correspondence

1. "For though we walk in the flesh, we do not war after the flesh: (For the weapons of our warfare are not carnal, but mighty through God to the pulling down of strongholds;) Casting down imaginations, and every high thing that exalts itself against the knowledge of God, and bringing into captivity every thought to the obedience of Christ," 2 Corinthians 10:3-5.
2. "But as he which hath called you is holy, so be ye holy in all manner of conversation; Because it is written, Be ye holy; for I am holy," 1 Peter 1:15-16, and "Let patience have her perfect work, that ye may be perfect and entire, wanting nothing," James 1:4.

with the High and Holy One;[1] upon fitting our minds for conversation and society with the wisest and purest spirits; upon providing for an immortal state, and upon the inheritance of joy and glory everlasting. It employs us in the most divine activities of promoting virtue, of performing kind and charitable deeds, of serving the public, and doing good to all men, which, when a man is exercised therein, these things do indeed render him of great worth and his life excellently valuable.

True religion is an employment most proper to us as reasonable men. For what more proper entertainment can our mind have than to be purifying and beautifying itself, to be keeping itself and its subordinate faculties in order, to be attending upon the management of thoughts, of passions, of words, and of actions that depend upon its governance?

It is an employment most beneficial to us, in the pursuit of which we greatly better ourselves and improve our condition, we are able to benefit and oblige others, and we procure a sound reputation and steady friendships. Hereby also we are able to avoid many irksome hazards, injuries, and annoyances. We do not, like those in the prophet, spend our labor for that which does not satisfy, nor

---

1. "Serve the Lord with fear, and rejoice with trembling. Kiss the Son, lest he be angry, and ye perish from the way, when his wrath is kindled but a little. Blessed are all they that put their trust in him," Psalms 2:11-12.

spend our money for that which is not food,[1] for *both* temporal prosperity and eternal felicity are the wages of the labor which we undertake herein.

It is an employment most constant, which never allows sloth or listlessness to creep in; it is incessantly busying all our faculties with earnest endeavors, even according to that profession of St. Paul, who declares the nature of true religion: "Herein always do I exercise myself, to have a conscience void of offence toward God and toward man," Acts 24:16. Upon which account, religion is called a fight[2] and a race,[3] implying by both the continual earnestness of attention and activity, which is to be spent thereupon.

It is altogether a sweet and gracious business, for it is a pious man's character, that "he delights greatly in God's commandments," Psalms 112:1; that "the commandments are not grievous to him," 1 John 5:3; that it is "his meat and drink to do God's will," John 4:34; that "God's words," or precepts, "are sweeter than honey to his taste," Psalms 119:103;

---

1. "Ho, everyone that thirsts, come ye to the waters, and he that has no money; come ye, buy, and eat; yea, come, buy wine and milk without money and without price. Wherefore do you spend money for that which is not bread? And your labor for that which satisfies not? Hearken diligently unto me, and eat ye that which is good, and let your soul delight itself in fatness. Incline your ear, and come unto me: hear, and your soul shall live," Isaiah 55:1-3.
2. "Fight the good fight of faith, lay hold on eternal life, whereunto thou art also called," 1 Timothy 6:12.
3. "Wherefore seeing we also are compassed about with so great a cloud of witnesses, let us lay aside every weight, and the sin which doth so easily beset us, and let us run with patience the race that is set before us," Hebrews 12:1.

and that the ways of religious "wisdom are ways of pleasantness, and all her paths are peace," Proverbs 3:17. Whereas all other employments are wearisome and so often become loathsome, the further we proceed in this employment, the more pleasant and satisfactory it grows. There is perpetually more substance of victory over the bad inclinations that trouble us from within and the strong temptations that assail us from without, which things, to combat, provide much satisfaction, and to master, breed inexpressible contentment. The sense also of God's love, the influences of his grace and comfort communicated in the performances of every devotion and duty, the satisfaction of a good conscience, the assured hope of reward, the foretastes of future bliss, altogether season and sweeten all the labors and all the difficulties undergone.

In fine, even the bare light of natural reasoning has discerned that, were it not for such matters as these to spend a man's care and pains upon, this would be a lamentable world to live in. There was, for example, an emperor as great and mighty as ever wielded a scepter upon earth, whose excellent virtue, coupled with wisdom—*inferior perhaps to none that any man had ever been endowed with without special inspiration*—qualified him with most advantage to examine and rightly to judge of things here; who, notwithstanding all the conveniences that his royal estate and prosperity might afford, which surely he had fully tasted and tried, did yet thus express his thoughts: Τι μοι ζην εν χοσμω χενω θεων, η προνοιας χενω, "What does it interest me to live in a world void of God, or void of Providence?"[1] To govern the greatest empire that ever was, in the deepest calm; to enjoy the largest abundance of wealth, of splendor, of respect, and of pleasure; to be loved, to be dreaded, to be served, to be adored by so many nations; to have the whole civil world obedient and yielding to his will and command, all these things seemed vain and idle, not worthy of a man's regard, affection, or choice, in the event that there were no God to worship, no providence to behold, and no piety to be exercised. Common sense has adjudged it so little worth the while to live without religion.

V.
Piety affords us the best friendships and the sweetest society.

It is a considerable benefit of piety that it affords us the best friendships and sweetest society. Man is framed for society and cannot live well without it[2]—many of his faculties would be useless, many of his appetites would rest unsatisfied in solitude. To have a wise and able friend, who is honest and good, and to whom we may have recourse upon all occasions for advice, for assistance, and for consolation is a great convenience in this life. And this benefit we owe to religion, which supplies us

---

1. M. Ant. ii, 11, vi, 10.
2. *Nullius boni sine socio jucunda possessio est.* Seneca, *Ep. vi.*

with various friendships of the best kind and that are most beneficial and sweetest to us.

Piety makes God our friend, a friend infinitely better than all friends, most affectionate and kind, most faithful and sure, most able, most willing, and ever most ready to perform every friendly office,[1] to yield advice in all our doubts, succor in all our needs, comfort in all our troubles, and satisfaction to all our desires. Unto him it ministers a free address upon all occasions, and with him it allows us continually a most sweet and pleasant communion.[2] The pious man always has the all-wise God to counsel him, to guide his actions and order his steps; he has the Almighty to protect, support, and relieve him, "For the Lord loves judgment, and forsakes not his saints; they are preserved forever," Psalms 37:28; he has the immense Goodness to commiserate and comfort him; unto him he is not only encouraged, but obliged to resort in need, "He will fulfill the desire of them that fear him: he also will hear their cry, and will save them," Psalms 145:19; upon him he may and he ought to discharge all his cares and burdens, "Humble yourselves therefore under the mighty hand of God, that he may exalt you in due time: casting all your care upon him; for he careth for you," 1 Peter 5:6-7.

---

1. "A good man obtains favor of the Lord," Proverbs 12:2.
2. "The eyes of the Lord are upon the righteous, and his ears are open unto their cry," Psalms 34:15; and "Behold, the eye of the Lord is upon them that fear him, upon them that hope in his mercy," Psalms 33:18.

It consequently engages all creatures in the world to be our friends or instruments of good to us, according to their several capacities, by the direction and disposal of God. All the servants of our great Friend will, in compliance with him, be serviceable to us: Job's friend promises him, upon condition of piety, "Thou shalt be in league with the stones of the field, and the beasts of the field shall be at peace with thee," Job 5:22. And God himself confirmed that promise, "In that day," says he in the prophet, "will I make a covenant for them with the beasts of the field, and with the fowls of heaven, and with the creeping things of the ground," Hoses 2:18. And again, "When you pass through the waters, I will be with you; and through the rivers, they shall not overflow you: when you walk through the fire, you shall not be burnt; neither shall the flame kindle upon you," Isaiah 42:2. And, "The sun shall not smite you by day, nor the moon by night," Psalms 121:6. "You shall tread upon the lion and adder, the young lion and the dragon shalt you trample under foot," Psalms 91:13. "They shall take up scorpions; and if they drink any deadly thing, it shall not hurt them," Mark 16:18—so our Lord promised to his disciples. Not only shall the heavens dispense their kindly influences, and the earth yield her plentiful stores, and all the elements discharge their natural and ordinary good offices; nor only the tame and sociable creatures shall upon this condition faithfully serve us;[1] but even the most wild, most fierce, most ravenous, most venomous creatures shall, if there be need, prove friendly and helpful, or at least harmless to us—as were the ravens to Elijah, "And the ravens brought him bread and flesh in the morning, and bread and flesh in the evening; and he drank of the brook," 1 Kings 17:6; the lions to Daniel,[2] the viper to St. Paul,[3] the fire to the three youths.[4]

But piety especially procures the friendship of the good angels, that mighty host of glorious and happy spirits; they all tenderly love the pious person, "there is joy in the presence of the angels of God over one sinner that repents," Luke 15:10; they are ever ready to serve and do him good, "Are they not all ministering spirits, sent forth to minister for them who shall be heirs of salvation?" Hebrews 1:14; to protect him from danger, to aid him in his undertakings, to rescue him from harm, "The angel of the Lord encamps round about them that fear him, and delivers them," Psalms

---

1. "The Lord shall open unto thee his good treasure, the heaven to give the rain unto thy land in his season, and to bless all the work of thine hand: and thou shalt lend unto many nations, and thou shalt not borrow," Deuteronomy 28:12.

2. Daniel 6.

3. "When Paul had gathered a bundle of sticks, and laid them on the fire, there came a viper out of the heat, and fastened on his hand. And when the barbarians saw the venomous beast hang on his hand, they said among themselves, No doubt this man is a murderer, whom, though he has escaped the sea, yet vengeance suffers not to live. And he shook off the beast into the fire, and felt no harm," Acts 28:3-5.

4. Daniel 3.

34:7; "For he shall give his angels charge over you, to keep you in all your ways," Psalms 91:11. What an honor, what a blessing is this, to have such an innumerable company of noble friends— the attendants and favorites of heaven—deeply concerned and constantly vigilant for our welfare!

Piety renders all sorts of men our friends. To good men it unites us in holy communion, the communion of brotherly love and hearty goodwill, attended with all the good offices they are able to perform; to other men it reconciles and endears us; for that innocent and inoffensive, courteous and benign, charitable and beneficent demeanor—such as piety requires and produces—are apt to draw out respect and affection from the worst men. For, *Vincit malos pertinax bonitas,* men hardly can persist enemies to him whom they perceive to be their friend.[1] And such is the pious man in disposition of mind and in effect toward all men when occasion serves, being sensible of his obligation to love all men and to "do good to all men" as he has opportunity, Galatians 6:10.[2] It assures and more strictly endears our friends to us. For, as it makes us hearty, faithful, constant friends to others, so it reciprocally ties others to us in the like sincerity and steadfastness of good will.

Piety reconciles enemies, for, "when a man's

---

1. Seneca, *Ep. vi.*
2. "As we have therefore opportunity, let us do good unto all men, especially unto them who are of the household of faith," Galatians 6:10.

ways do please the Lord, he makes his enemies to be at peace with him," Proverbs 16:7. It has a natural efficacy to that purpose and divine blessing promotes it.

By it all conversation becomes tolerable, gratifying, and useful. For a pious man is not easily disturbed with any crossness or perverseness, any infirmity or impertinence of those he converses with; he can bear the weaknesses and the failings of his associates; he can by wholesome reflections upon all occurrences find that which works for his good in all; and he pleases himself in all by striving after a clear conscience before God and men.

In fine, piety renders a man a true friend and a good companion to himself; he is satisfied in himself and able to converse freely and pleasantly with his own thoughts. It is the lack of pious inclinations and dispositions, that solitude—a thing which sometimes cannot be avoided and that often should be embraced—is to most men so irksome and tedious, that men do carefully shun themselves and fly from their own thoughts, they decline all converse with their own souls and hardly dare look upon their own hearts and consciences. Whereupon men become as aliens from home, wholly unacquainted with themselves, and most ignorant of their own nearest concernments, being, least of all, no faithful friend or pleasant companion to themselves—for refuge and ease they run at all times into idle or lewd conversation where they disorder and defile themselves. But the pious man is never less alone than when alone: his solitude and retirement is not only tolerable, but commonly the most grateful and fruitful part of his life. He can at all times and with much pleasure and greater advantage, converse with himself,[1] digesting and marshalling his thoughts, his affections, his purposes into good order; searching and discussing his heart, reflecting on his past ways; enforcing his former good resolutions and framing new ones; inquiring after edifying truths and extending his meditations toward the best and most sublime objects,[2] raising his hopes and warming his affections towards spiritual and heavenly things; asking himself pertinent questions, and resolving occasional doubts concerning his practice. In fine, conversing with himself in devotion; contemplating, with admiration and love the divine perfections displayed in the works of nature, of providence, and of grace; praising God for his excellent benefits and mercies; confessing his defects and offences; entreating against wrath and imploring pardon, with grace and ability to amend; and praying for the supply of all his wants. All of which undertakings yield both inconceivable benefits and inexpressible comfort. So that solitude, which is so offensive to our common nature, is to the pious man extremely commodious and comfortable, and

1. "I will bless the Lord, who hath given me counsel: my reins *(my heart)* also instruct me in the night seasons," Psalms 16:7.
2. "Meditate upon these things; give thyself wholly to them; that thy profiting may appear to all," 1 Timothy 4:15.

is a great advantage particularly to piety, and the last advantage that I shall mention.

So many, many more vastly great and precious advantages—*more than I can express*—do accrue from piety, so that, well may we conclude and say with St. Paul:

"Godliness is profitable for all things."
1 Timothy 4:8

It remains that, if we are wise and if we do not yet have godliness engrafted in us, we should labor to acquire it. If we have it, we should endeavor to improve it by constant exercise,[1] and that, to the praise of God, the good of our neighbor, and our own comfort in the faith of Jesus Christ. These all, we may effectually perform, as the Almighty God in mercy grants according to his grace, through Jesus Christ our Lord, to whom be all glory and praise forever. Amen.

---

1. "Exercise yourself rather unto godliness," 1 Timothy 4:7.

GODLINESS
IS
PROFITABLE
FOR ALL THINGS

PART III

Evidences from other sources

I. Rev. John Newton
True religion is necessary to the enjoyment of this present life

II. Rev. Robert Leighton
Happiness cannot be found in earthly things

III. St. John Chrysostom
On the value of godliness

I. REV. JOHN NEWTON

(1725-1807)

Excerpt from The Letters of John Newton,
Vol. 1, Letter XXXVIII

True religion is necessary to the enjoyment of this present life

I. REV. JOHN NEWTON

(1725-1807)

Excerpt from The Letters of John Newton,
Vol. 1, Letter XXXVIII

True religion is necessary to the enjoyment of this present life

To a Merry Friend.

Dear Sir,

Though I truly love you and have no reason to doubt the reality of your friendship to me, yet I cannot but think that, notwithstanding our mutual regard and my frequent attempts to be witty (if I could) for your diversion, there is a something in most of my letters—which I cannot and dare not wholly suppress—that disgusts and wearies you, and makes you less inclined to keep up a frequent communication than you would be otherwise. Rather than lose you completely, I will, in general, spare you as much as I can, but at present you must bear with me and allow me full scope. You have given me a challenge that I do not know how to pass up, and since you so far justify my preaching as to condescend to preach in your own way yourself, permit me on this occasion to preach again and to take some passages in your letter for my text.

In the present debate I will accept your compliment and suppose myself to be, as you say, a man of sense. You allow, then, that *all* the sense is not on your side. This, indeed, you cannot deny, for whatever becomes of me, it is needless to tell you that Hale, Boyle, and other great names I could mention, were men of as great sagacity and judgment, had as good opportunities, and took as much pains to be informed of the truth, as any of the advocates for infidelity can claim to. And you cannot, with any modesty or consistency, absolutely determine that they had not as good grounds for thinking themselves right as you can have for concluding that they were wrong.

But declining to add the advantage of human authority, I am content that the point should rest between you and me. And here I beg you to observe, that I have one evident advantage over you in judging, namely, that I have experienced the good and evil on *both* sides, and you only on *one*. If you were to send me an inventory of your pleasures, how charmingly your time runs on, and how dexterously it is divided between the coffee-house, the playhouse, the card-table, and the tavern, with intervals of balls, concerts, etc., I would answer that most of these I have tried and tried again, and know the utmost they can yield, and have seen enough of the rest, most heartily to despise them all.

Setting religion entirely out of the question, I profess that I would rather be a worm crawling upon the ground than to bear the name of man upon the poor terms of whiling away my life in an insipid round of such insignificant and unmanly trifles. I will use your own expression—I believe you to be a person of sense, but alas, how you prostitute your talents and capacity! How far below your ability do you function if you find no higher purpose in life than childish dissipations and the more serious business of rising early and sitting up late to amass money that you may be able to enlarge your expenses! I can say surely that while I lived in these things, I found them unsatisfying and empty to the last degree. The only advantage they afforded—miserable are they who are forced to deem it an advantage—was that they often relieved me from the trouble and burden of thinking. If you get from them any other pleasures than these, they are such as must be evil and inconvenient, even upon your own design, and therefore my friendship will not allow me to bring them into the account. I am willing to hope you do not stoop still lower in pursuit of satisfaction. Thus far we stand upon even ground. You know all that a life of pleasure can give, and I know it in like manner.

On the other hand, if I were to attempt to explain to you the source and streams of *my* best pleasures, such as a comfortable assurance of the pardon of my sins, a constant communion with the God who made heaven and earth, a calm reliance on the divine providence, the cheering prospect of a better life in a better world, with the pleasing foretastes of heaven in my soul, and if I were to *or could* tell you the pleasure I often find in reading the Scripture, in the exercise of prayer, and in that sort of preaching and conversation which you despise, I doubt not but that you would think as poorly of my happiness as I do of yours. But here lies the difference, my dear friend—you condemn that which you have never tried. You know no more of these things than a blind man does of colors, and, notwithstanding all your increase and prosperity, I defy you to be able at all times to satisfy yourself that things may not possibly be as I have represented them.

Besides, what do I lose upon my design that should make me so worthy of your pity? Have you a quicker relish in the prudent use of temporal comforts? Do you think I do not eat my food with as much pleasure as you can do, though perhaps with less cost and variety? Is your sleep sounder than mine? Have not I as much satisfaction in social life? It is true, to join much with the gay, fluttering tribe, who spend their days in laughter and song and verse, is equally contrary to my duty and inclination. But I have friends and acquaintances as well as you. Among the many who favor me with their esteem and friendship, there are some who are persons of sense, learning, wit, and—what perhaps may weigh as much with you—of fortune and distinction. And if you should say, "Yes, but they are all enthusiasts like yourself," you would say nothing to the purpose, but the contrary, since according to your own maxim that "happiness is according to opinion," it cannot be an objection to have my acquaintance to my own taste. This much said regarding the brighter side of your situation—or let me add one thing more, as I know you have thoughts of marriage: do you think that if you should enter into this relation, your principles are calculated to make you more happy in it than I am? You are well acquainted with our family-life here. Do you propose to know more of the peace and heartfelt joy of domestic union than I have known, and continue to know to this hour? I wish you may equal us, and if you do, we shall still be as before, but upon even ground. I need not become a Deist to enjoy the best and the most that this life can afford.

But I need not tell you that the present life is not made up of pleasurable incidents only. Pain, sickness, losses, disappointments, injuries, and affronts with men will more or less and at one time or another be our lot. And can you bear these trials better than I? You will not pretend to it. Let me appeal to you: How often do you toss and disquiet yourself like a wild bull in a net when things cross your expectations? As your thoughts are more engrossed by what you see, you must be more keenly sensible of what you feel. You cannot view these trials as appointed by a wise and heavenly Father in subservience to your good; you cannot taste the sweetness of his promises nor feel the secret supports of his strength in an hour of affliction; you cannot so cast your burden and care upon him as to find a sensible relief to your spirit thereby; nor can you see his hand engaged and employed in effecting your deliverance. Of these things you know no more than of the art of flying, but I seriously assure you, and I believe my testimony will go further with you than my judgment, that they are realities and that I have found them to be so. When my worldly concerns have been most thorny and discouraging, I have once and again felt the most of that peace which the world can neither give nor take away.

However, I will state the case more to your present experiences. You do pretty well among your friends—but how do you like being alone? Would you not give something for that happy secret that could enable you to pass a rainy day pleasantly, without the assistance of business, company, or amusement? Would it not mortify you greatly to travel for a week in an unfrequented road, where you should meet with no lively incidents to recruit and raise your spirits? Alas! What a poor scheme of pleasure is yours that will not support an interval of reflection.

What you have heard is true; I have a few friends who meet at my house once every two weeks and we spend an hour or two in worshipping the God who made us. And can this move your indignation or your compassion? Does it show a much nobler spirit, a more refined way of thinking to live altogether without God in the world? If I held a card game at those times it would not displease you. How can you, as a person of sense, avoid being shocked at your own unhappy prejudice? But I remember how it was once with myself, and thus forebear to wonder. May he who has opened my eyes, open yours! He alone can do it. I do not expect to convince you by anything that I can say as of myself, but if he is pleased to make use of me as his instrument then you will be convinced. How would I then rejoice! I would rejoice to be useful to anyone, but especially to you whom I dearly love. May God show you your true self and your true state, then you will attentively listen to what you now disdain to hear about God's goodness in providing redemption and pardon for the chiefest of sinners, through him who died upon the cross for sins not his own.

II. REV. ROBERT LEIGHTON

(1611–1684)

Excerpt from The Works of Rev. Robert Leighton, Vol. 2, Lecture IV

Happiness cannot be found in earthly things

II. REV. ROBERT LEIGHTON

(1611-1684)

Excerpt from The Works of Rev. Robert Leighton, Vol. 2, Lecture IV

Happiness cannot be found in earthly things

We are all in quest of one thing, but almost all of us search off the right road. Therefore, to be sure, the longer and the more quickly we travel along a wrong path, the further we depart from the object of our desires. And, if it is so, we can speak or think of nothing more proper and seasonable, than of inquiring about the only right way, whereby we may all come "to see the bright fountain of goodness."[1]

Remember that on *(a previous)* occasion, we proposed the most important of all questions, viz., that concerning our ultimate end or the way to discover true happiness. To true happiness, we asserted that all mankind aspires with a natural and

---

1. *Boni fontem visere lucidum.*

therefore a constant and uniform ardor, or rather, we supposed that all are sufficiently acquainted with this happiness, nay, really do or at least may feel it within themselves if they thoroughly know themselves. For, this is the end of the labors of men and to this tend all their toils. This is the general aim of all, not only of the sharp-sighted but of the bleary-eyed and short-sighted, nay, even of those that are quite blind, who, although they cannot see the mark they propose to themselves, yet they are in hopes of reaching it at last. This is only to say that although their ideas of felicity are very confused and imperfect, yet they all desire happiness in the obvious sense of the word.

We have also observed that this term, in its general sense, imports that full and perfect good which is suited to intelligent nature.[1] It is not to be doubted that the felicity of the Deity, as well as his being, is in himself and from himself. But our inquiry is concerning our own happiness. We also positively determined *(on another occasion)* that there is some blessed end suited and adapted to our nature, and that this can by no means be denied. For, since all parts of the universe have proper ends suited and adapted to their natures, the very idea that the most noble and excellent creature upon the earth might be deficient in this and was therefore created in vain, would be so great an absurdity and such a deformity in the whole fabric, as to be unworthy of the supreme and all-wise Creator, that it can by

---

1. Πρωτον τε, εχατον τε, και μεγιστον καλον.

no means be admitted nor imagined. This point being settled, viz., that there is some determinate good that, in the possession of it, the mind of man may be fully satisfied and at perfect rest, we now proceed to inquire what this good is and where it may be found.

The first thing—and at the same time a very considerable step towards the discovery of this good—will be to show where and in what things this perfect good is *not* to be found, not only because, this point being settled, it will be easier to determine wherein it actually consists, but because the latter will naturally flow from the former and because, as has been observed, we shall find the far greater part of mankind pursuing vain shadows and phantoms of happiness, and throughout their whole lives, we shall see them wandering into a great variety of by-paths, seeking the way to make a proper improvement of life, almost always hunting for that chief good where it is not to be found. They must first be recalled from this rambling and fruitless course before they can possibly be directed into the right road. I shall not spin out this negative proposition by dividing the subject of it into several branches and insisting separately upon every one of them, but by considering all these errors and mistakes, both vulgar and practical, speculative and philosophical, however numerous they may be, as comprehended under one general heading, and fully remove them all by one single proposition, which, with divine assistance, I shall explain to you in this lecture.

The Proposition

The proposition is that human felicity or that full and complete good that is suited to the nature of man is not to be found in the earth, nor in earthly things.

Now, what if, instead of further proof or illustration, I should only say:

If this perfect felicity is to be found within this visible world or the scope of this earthly life, I pray, let him who has discovered it, stand forth; whoever can, let him tell what star of whatever magnitude, what constellation or combination of stars, has so favorable an aspect and so benign an influence, or what is that singular good or assemblage of good things in this earth that can confer a happy life upon mankind. All things that have hitherto attracted the eyes of men like bright stars, having vanished in a few days, have only proved themselves to be comets. They have proved not only of no benign but of even a pernicious influence, according to the saying, Ουδεις γαρ κομητες οστις ου κακον φερει, *"There is no comet but that which brings some evil along with it."* All that have ever lived during so many ages that the world has hitherto lasted, noble and ignoble, learned and unlearned, fools and wise men, have gone in search of happiness—has ever any one of them all in times past, or is there any one at this day that has said, Εὑρηκα,[1] *"I have found it"*?

Different men have given different definitions and descriptions of happiness and, according to their various turns of mind, have painted it in a great variety of shapes. But, since the creation of the world, there has not been so much as one who ever pretended to say, *Here it is, I have it and have attained the full possession of it.* Even those from whom most was to be expected—men of the utmost acuteness and most properly qualified for such researches—after all their labor and industry, have acknowledged their disappointment and have confessed that they had not found it.

But it would be a wonder indeed that there should be such a good suited to human nature and to which mankind were born, and yet that a share of it never fell to any single individual among men, unless it is said, that the things of life, in this respect, resemble the speculations of the schools and that, as they talk about objects of knowledge that were never known, so there is some good that is attainable by men but that was never actually attained.

But to look a little more closely into this matter, we take a transient view of the various periods of life. Infants are so far from attaining to happiness that they have not yet arrived at any

---

1. Εὑρηκα, that is, eureka, "I have found it!"

measure of experience of human life. Yet, if infants are compared with those of riper years they are, in an improper sense, with regard to two things, namely, innocence and ignorance, happier than men. For there is nothing that years add to infancy, so invariably and in so great abundance, as guilt and pollution; and the experience and knowledge of the world that these give us do not so much improve the head, as they vex and distress the heart. So that the great man represented in the tragedy embracing his infant, who knew nothing of his own misery, seems to have had some reason to say, Το γνωναι μηδεν εστιν ηδιστος βιος, "*That those who know nothing enjoy the happiest life.*" And to be sure, what we come to understand through our progress from infancy to youth is that we become more exposed to the miseries of life and, as we increase in the knowledge of things, our pains and torments are also increased; for as the young are put to employments and education, they are subjected to punishments, rods and chastisements under the power of parents and instructors, which often becomes a kind of petty tyranny, so that, when the yoke is lightened it still seems hard to be borne, as it is above their ability to bear it, thwarts their wishes and inclinations, and encroaches upon their beloved liberty.

Youth, however, in full possession of liberty, for the most part ceases to be master of itself, nor can the emancipated youth be truly said to be delivered from its former misery, so much as having exchanged it for a worse—even that very liberty. It leaves the harbor, only to sail through quicksands and sirens, and when both of these are passed, it launches out into the deep sea and alas, to whatever various fate it is there exposed! How many contrary winds does it meet with! How many storms threatening it with shipwreck! How many shocks has it to endure from avarice, ambition, and envy, either in consequence of the violent stirring of those passions within itself or fierce attacks by them from without! Amidst all these tempests, the ship is either early overwhelmed or broken by storms, and is ultimately worn out by age.

Nor does it much signify what state of life one enters into, or what rank he holds in human society, for all forms of business and conditions of life, however different you may suppose them to be, are exposed to a great variety of troubles and distresses, some to pressures more numerous and more grievous than others, but all to a great many in general and every one to some peculiar to itself. If you devote yourself to ease and retirement, you cannot avoid the reproach and uneasiness that constantly attends an indolent, a useless, and lazy life. If you engage in business, whatever it may be, whether you become a merchant, a soldier, a farmer, or a lawyer, you always meet with toil and hazard, and often with heavy misfortunes and losses. The single life exposes a man to solitude; marriage, to solicitude and cares. Without learning, you will appear plain and unpolished; but on the other hand, the study of letters is a matter of immense labor, and, for the most part, brings in but very little, either with regard to the knowledge you acquire by it, or the conveniences of life it procures; and so are all things. You find the Greek and Latin poets lamenting the calamities of life, and at great length, in many parts of their works: nor do they exaggerate in the least, but even fall short of the truth and only enumerate a few evils out of many.

But now, leaving the various periods and conditions of life, let us, with great brevity, run through those things which are looked upon to be the greatest blessings in it, and see whether any of them can make it completely happy:

Can happiness be expected from exterior beauty? No, but this has rendered many miserable, and never made one happy. For suppose it to be sometimes accompanied with innocence, yet it is of a fading and perishing nature[1] and will become "the sport of time or disease."[2]

Can happiness be expected from riches? Surely no, for how little of them does the owner possess, even supposing his wealth to be ever so great! What a small part of them does he use or enjoy himself! And what has he of the rest but the pleasure of

1. "Favor is deceitful, and beauty is vain: but a woman that fears the Lord, she shall be praised," Proverbs 31:30.
2. Χρονου η νοσου παιγνιον.

seeing them with his eyes?[1] Let his table be loaded with the greatest variety of delicious dishes, yet he fills his stomach from one, and if he has a hundred beds, he lies but in one of them.

Can the kingdoms, thrones, and scepters of this world confer happiness? No, we learn from the histories of every age that not a few have been thrown down by sudden and unexpected revolutions, and of those, not such as were void of command or courage but men of great and extraordinary abilities. And of those who met with no such misfortunes, yet were they still far enough from happiness, as is very plain from the situation of their affairs and in many cases, from their own confessions. The saying of Augustus is well known: "I wish I had never been married, and had died childless." And the expression of Severus at his death, "I became all things, and yet it does not profit me."[2] But the most noted saying of all, and that which best deserves to be known, is that of the wisest and most flourishing king, as well as the greatest preacher, who, having exactly accounted all the advantages of his exalted dignity and royal opulence, found this to be the sum total of all, and left it on record for the inspection of posterity and future ages, "Vanity of vanities, saith the preacher; all is vanity," Ecclesiastes 12:8.

---

1. "When goods increase, they are increased that eat them: and what good is there to the owners thereof, saving the beholding of them with their eyes?" Ecclesiastes 5:11.
2. Παντα εγενομην και ου λυσιτελει.

Granting that all of this may be true with regard to all of the external advantages of men, but may not happiness be found in the internal goods of the mind—such as wisdom and virtue? Suppose this is conceded, yet, that we should grant that these may confer perfect felicity, they must of necessity be perfect themselves. Now, show me the man, who, even in his own judgment, has attained to perfection in wisdom and virtue: even those who were accounted the wisest and were actually so, yet these all acknowledged that they knew nothing, nor was there one among the most approved philosophers, whose virtues were not allayed with many blemishes.

Something of the same must be said of piety and true religion, which, though it is the beginning of felicity and tends directly to perfection, yet, while we yet remain in this earth it is not full and complete in itself, "For now we see through a glass, darkly," 1 Corinthians 13:12, and it cannot make its possessors perfectly happy, "Not as though I had already attained, either were already perfect: but I follow after, if that I may apprehend that for which also I am apprehended of Christ Jesus," Philippians 3:12. The knowledge of the most exalted minds is very obscure and almost quite dark, and their practice of virtue remains but weak and imperfect, yet in imperfection, that which is perfect is of the power of God:

"For God, who commanded the light to

shine out of darkness, hath shined in our hearts, to give the light of the knowledge of the glory of God in the face of Jesus Christ. But we have this treasure in earthen vessels, that the excellency of the power may be of God, and not of us," 2 Corinthians 4:6-7.

And indeed, who can have the boldness to boast of perfection in this respect when he hears the great Apostle complaining of the law of the flesh and pathetically exclaiming, "Who shall deliver me from this body of death?" Romans 7:24. Besides, though wisdom and virtue, or piety, were perfect, so long as we have earthly bodies, we would have to have at the same time all bodily advantages, in order to live in perfect felicity.

Since these things are so, we must raise our minds higher, "Looking unto Jesus the author and finisher of our faith; who for the joy that was set before him endured the cross, despising the shame, and is set down at the right hand of the throne of God," Hebrews 12:2.

To set our hearts upon the perishing goods of this wretched life and its muddy pleasures, is not the happiness of men, but of hogs. And if pleasure is but dirt, all other things of this world are but smoke. And if these worldly things were the only happinesses proposed to the desires and hopes of men, it would not have been so great a privilege to have been born. Be therefore advised and beware of this poisonous cup. Turn that part of your composition that is divine to God its Creator and Father, without whom we can neither be happy, nor indeed be at all.

"If ye then be risen with Christ, seek those things which are above, where Christ sitteth on the right hand of God. Set your affection on things above, not on things on the earth," Colossians 3:1-2.

III. ST. JOHN CHRYSOSTOM

Excerpt from The Homilies of St. John Chrysostom, Archbishop of Constantinople,

On the Epistle Of St. Paul the Apostle to the Romans, Homily I

On the value of godliness

III. ST. JOHN CHRYSOSTOM

Excerpt from The Homilies of St. John Chrysostom,
Archbishop of Constantinople,

On the Epistle Of St. Paul the Apostle to the
Romans, Homily I

(This an enlarged passage from Chrysostom in the place
referenced by our author on pg. 77; it is included here for
context and further commentary.)

On the value of godliness

Note how free the mind of Paul is from all flattery; for when conversing with the Romans, who were seated as it were upon a sort of summit of the whole world, he attaches no more to them than to the other nations, nor does he on the score of their being then in power and ruling, say, that they have in spiritual things also any advantage. But as (he means) we preach to all the nations, so do we to you, numbering them with Scythians and Thracians. . . . And this he does to take down their high spirit (κενων το φυσημα), and to prostrate the swelling vanity of their minds, and to teach them to honor others alike to themselves: and so he proceeds to speak upon this very point.

For if in Christ Jesus there is neither bond nor free, much less is there king and private man. . . . For since among them which believed, it was likely that there would be some of the consuls (υπατων; Ben. *consulares*) and rulers as well as poor and common men, casting aside the inequality of ranks, he writes to them all under one appellation. But if in things which are more needful and which are spiritual, all things are set forth as common both to slaves and to free, for instance, the love from God, the calling, the Gospel, the adoption, the grace, the peace, the sanctification, all things else. . . . On this ground, I presume, from the very outset, this blessed Apostle, after casting out this mischievous disease, conducts them to the mother of blessings—humble-mindedness. This made servants better, since they learned that they would receive no harm from their servitude, while they had the true freedom; this would incline masters to be gentle, as being instructed that they have no advantage in being free, unless the commodity of faith has the primary place given it.

And that you may learn that he was not doing this to work confusion, by destroying all things, but still knew the best distinction, he wrote not simply to all that were in Rome, but with a definition added, "beloved of God." For this is the best discrimination, and shows from what source the sanctification was. From where then was the sanctification? From love. . . . It was no small war which Christ put an end to, but indeed one varying and of every kind and of a long season (τοικιλον και ταντοδαπον); and this not from our labors, but through his grace. Since then love presented us with grace, and grace with peace, having set them down in the due order of an address, he prays over them that they may abide perpetual and unmoved, so that no other war may again be fanned into flames, and beseeches him that gave, to keep these things firmly settled, saying as follows, "Grace be unto you and peace from God our Father, and the Lord Jesus Christ." . . . Strange! How mighty is the love of God! We which were enemies and disgraced, have all at once become saints and sons. For when he calls him Father, he shows them to be sons; and when he says sons, he has unveiled the whole treasure of blessings.

Let us then keep showing a conversation worthy of the gift, and hold on in peace and holiness. For other dignities are but for a time, and are brought to an end along with this life present, and may be bought with money—from which one might say that they are not dignities at all but names of dignities only, having their strength in the investiture of fine array and the servility of attendants—but *this* as having been given of God, the gift of sanctification and adoption, is not destroyed even by death, but even here makes men conspicuous, and departs also with us upon our journey to the life to come.

For he that holds on in the adoption, and keeps an exact watch upon his holiness, is much brighter and more happy even than he that is arrayed with the diadem itself, and has the purple; and has the delight of abundant peace in the present life and is nourished with good hopes, and has no ground for worry and disturbance, but enjoys constant pleasure; for as for good spirits and joy, it is not greatness of power, not abundance of wealth, not pomp of authority, not strength of body, not sumptuousness of the table, not the adorning of dresses, nor any other of the things in man's reach that ordinarily produces them, but spiritual success and a good conscience alone. And he that has this cleansed, even though he is clad in rags and struggling with famine, is of better spirits than they that live so softly. So too he that is conscious of wicked deeds, even though he may gather to himself all men's goods, is the most wretched of all men.

For this cause Paul, living in continual hunger and nakedness and being scourged every day, was joyful and went more softly than they that were then emperors. But Ahab, though a king and indulging in a sumptuous luxury, when he had done that one sin, groaned and was out of spirits, and his countenance was fallen both before the sin and after the sin.

If then we wish to enjoy pleasure, above all other

things, let us shun wickedness and follow after virtue; since it is not in the nature of things for one to have a share thereof, that is, of the enjoyment of pleasure, on any other terms, even if we were mounted upon the king's throne itself.

Wherefore also Paul saith, "But the fruit of the Spirit is love, joy, peace," Galatians 5:22. This fruit then let us keep growing by us, that we may be in the fruition of joy here, and may obtain the kingdom to come, by the grace and love towards man of our Lord Jesus Christ, through whom and with whom, be glory to the Father and to the Holy Spirit, now and always, even unto all ages. Amen.

"By manifestation of the truth commending ourselves to every man's conscience in the sight of God." 2 Corinthians 4:2

HAIL & FIRE
www.hailandfire.com

Other Paperbacks

The Mute Christian *under the Smarting Rod*
by Rev. Thomas Brooks (1659)
Hail & Fire (2011)
ISBN-13 978-0-9828043-3-9

The Marriage Ring
or How to Make Home Happy
by Rev. John Angell James *(1842)*
With a sermon entitled "Right to Divorce & Remarriage in the Case of Adultery" by John Owen
Hail & Fire (2010)
ISBN-13 978-0-9828043-2-2

Gehazi, The Sinner Detected
A Puritan style Sermon on Temptation and Secret Sins: "Be sure your sin will find you out." Numbers 32
Hail & Fire (2010 Illustrated Edition)
ISBN-13 978-0-9828043-1-5

The Martyrdom of a People:
or The Vaudois of Piedmont and their History
by Henry Fliedner *(1914)*
Hail & Fire (2010 Illustrated Edition)
ISBN-13 978-0-9828043-0-8

The Huguenot Galley Slaves
from the Memoirs of Jean Martielhe (1759)
Hail & Fire (2011 Illustrated Edition)
ISBN-13 978-0-9828043-4-6

www.ingramcontent.com/pod-product-compliance
Lightning Source LLC
Chambersburg PA
CBHW061727020426
42331CB00006B/1132

* 9 780982 804353 *